Country Boys, Country Love

Brinx/Kömmerling

Country Boys, Country Love

Aus dem Deutschen
von Sally-Ann Spencer

Thienemann

For the best parents in the world
Who taught us
What village life is like!

Heaven and Hell

I'll push them off the balcony, every last one of them. The stupid flowerpots will hit the ground with a bang, seven **storeys** down. The same kind of bang that went off in my head when my parents told me their brilliant idea. The kind of bang that **tore** my **heart apart**.

Mum loves her plants. She loves any bit of greenery that survives on our city-centre balcony. She **shrieks with delight** as soon as anything **sprouts** there – even **stinging nettles** or **crappy** little plants.

"Crappy little plants? What's wrong with you, Annika?" I **brace** myself **for** the lecture. "Plants are living creatures like you and me. They grow, develop and make oxygen for us to breathe!"

Yawn. I know exactly what's coming. Mum

---

storey – Stockwerk;
to tear apart – zerreißen;
to shriek with delight – vor Begeisterung schreien;
to sprout – sprießen; stinging nettle – Brennnessel;
crappy – beschissen; to brace oneself for – sich wappnen für etwas; to yawn – gähnen

spends hours **fussing and cooing** over her oxygen-emitting plants, sprinkling them with home-made **potions** from a tiny watering-can with a metre-long **spout**. She talks to them, too. Well, naturally. Plants are living creatures so they must have ears. I'm waiting for the day when they finally talk back.

Mum: "That's right, and now I'm going to give you a bit of water to make you big and strong."

Plant: "I wouldn't bother if I were you. No **offence**, but we're on the seventh storey above a main road. We'll never grow strong."

And they don't. I'll teach them how to fly, though. For the first and last time these incredible living plants will fly through the air and explode on the **pavement**. There won't be anything left. It's time Mum knew how it feels to have a broken heart.

If the last few days have taught me anything, it's this: *never* sleep over at your best friend's house, *never* go on holiday and *never ever* stay a night away from home. Parents cause trouble as soon as they're alone. Turn your back for a second and they'll **shove** you out of seventh heaven and straight into hell.

---

fussing and cooing – *hier:* rupfen und zupfen; potion – Tinktur, Gebräu; spout – Ausgießer; offence – Beleidigung; pavement – Bürgersteig; to shove – schubsen

The school ski holiday – that was seventh heaven. All three classes went to Saalbach, and *he* came, too. That's Alex the new boy in 8b. His mother is Indian, which explains his fiery dark eyes. He can give you a **searing** look that turns you into a **pile of ash** and **scatters** you on the wind. The first time he looked at me, I needed 30 minutes to recover and get back to being me: Annika Weber, no. 64 Balderstraße, 80469 Munich. But was I really me? No, I was in love. Naturally Suse saw it right away.

"Not you as well," she **groaned**, looking at me pityingly.

Sure, I wasn't the only one who'd fallen for Alex, but four, five or maybe ten rivals are nothing compared to four, five or ten million. You see, Suse is in love with Robbie Williams. Her whole room is covered in photos. Robbie from the front, from behind, from the side, laughing, crying, singing or with his trousers down. We've spent entire weeks imagining what we'll do when he sings in Munich – we'll trick his army of bodyguards and sneak into his hotel. As soon as Robbie sees Suse, he'll be overcome with emotion and realize that she's the girl for him.

"Did you see his eyes?" I **drooled after** Alex.

---

searing – glühend; pile of ash – Häufchen Asche;
to scatter – zerstreuen; to groan – stöhnen;
to drool after sb – jmdm. hinterherschmachten

"Not as good as Robbie's," said Suse with a **frown**.

"A million times better!"

"Huh! No one's got better eyes than Robbie. Not even close!"

You can't argue with Suse where Robbie is concerned. She's crazy about him – totally starstruck. He's too old for me, but Suse **fancies** our German teacher and he's over 30, which is as good as dead. At least it means we don't like the same guys though. All Alex and Robbie have in common is that they both have lots of fans. Alex's admirers are always **clustered round** him, staring into his fiery eyes, hanging on every word that leaves his beautiful lips, and **vying** to get his attention.

How was I **supposed to** get near him? There was no way I was going to join his fan club, lining up with all the other girls who **melted** in his presence, **dissolving** into a nameless, faceless mass.

As soon as we were told to sign up for ski lessons in Saalbach, I knew what I had to do. I scanned the lists and **seized my chance**. Alex was in the top group, the class for hard-core skiers. All the others

---

frown – Stirnrunzeln; to fancy sb – jmdn. zum Küssen finden; to cluster round – sich drängen um; vying – wetteifernd; to be supposed to do sth – etwas tun sollen; to melt – schmelzen; to dissolve – (sich) auflösen; to seize one's chance – seine Chance ergreifen

were boys – not a single girl in sight. I **whipped out** my pen and signed my name under his.

"Do you want to kill yourself or something?" asked Suse, entering her name in the intermediate column for losers. I should have been in that group, too.

"Imagine Robbie was a hard-core skier!" I said, **tracing over** my signature to show my determination. I had to get closer to Alex, even if it meant skiing down a black **run** or sliding over **moguls**. If anything happened to me, this signature would be my final testament, proof of my undying love. My eyes **moistened** at the thought of it.

I had tears in my eyes the following day, too, but at that stage it had nothing to do with being sentimental. It had snowed throughout the night and it was snowing that morning. Everything looked white as white, like a nasty case of snow-blindness. An icy wind swept the mountain, **rocking** the gondola from side to side. It was worse than being at the **fairground**. I felt sick.

Everyone was **muffled** in their warmest clothes except me. How would Alex fall in love with me if all he could see was my nose? I don't even like my

---

to whip out – herausholen; to trace over – nachziehen; run – Piste; mogul – Buckel; to moisten – feucht werden; to rock – schaukeln; fairground – Rummelplatz; to be muffled – eingemummelt sein

nose. It's Dad's **fault** for giving me his potato nose and not Mum's elegant straight one.

"Are you going to be warm enough?" asked Reichel, our sports teacher.

"Hey, don't worry about me – I never get cold." That was the first lie. I told another one when he asked about our skiing skills. The others had practically skied since birth, including Alex. I didn't want to make a bad impression. "I learned to ski before I could walk," I joked. Actually, I learned to ski last year with Suse and her mum.

The gondola **spat** us **out** at the top of the mountain, and I suddenly understood why my parents preferred beach holidays to ski trips. First I was **paralysed** with cold, then I felt hot all over as I looked down the black run. A black run with moguls.

"Let's start with something nice and easy," shouted Reichel. "Off you go!"

Nice and easy? Did he say easy?!

Reichel set off downhill, followed by the boys. I headed after them. A **clumsy** left turn, a pathetic right turn, and my skis were out of control. I slammed down and **sprained** my thumb.

"At least it wasn't your right hand," said Suse

---

fault – Schuld, Fehler; to spit out – ausspucken;
paralysed – erstarrt, gelähmt;
clumsy – plump, ungeschickt; to sprain – verstauchen

when I got back from the doctor's. She always tries to look on the bright side. If she lost both legs in an accident, she'd probably be **grateful** for not having to do gym.

Sadly, I couldn't see anything **remotely** positive about the situation. My left thumb had swollen to the size of a **cucumber** and was hurting like hell. I'd embarrassed myself in front of the others and I'd ruined my chances of getting to know Alex. For the rest of the week I'd be sitting around in the chalet, **twiddling my thumbs**. Actually, I only had one thumb to twiddle – the left one was sprained.

But was Alex even worth my efforts? He hadn't looked at me in the gondola. He was too busy staring out of the window, **deafening** himself with his iPod. And he hadn't exactly looked worried when I fell over. He'd hung back while I lay in the snow, thumb swelling by the second, and let the others take charge.

I still went bright red when Fat Mario came running with the news. "You'll never believe it," he called out in his choirboy voice, "Reichel's given Alex a black-eye!"

---

grateful – dankbar; remote – entfernt;
cucumber – Salatgurke;
to twiddle one's thumbs – Däumchen drehen;
to deafen – taub machen, *hier:* zudröhnen

"He's done what?" I **gasped**, staring at Mario in surprise.

"They were in the pool," **panted** Mario, out of breath from the **exertion**. "Reichel swims like a **pro**. He didn't see Alex was in the way. Bang! He punched him right in the eye!"

"Lucky it wasn't his throat. That could have been **fatal** ... " Like I said, Suse always looks on the bright side.

I went even redder when Alex came up to me on the balcony the next day. The clouds had emptied themselves of snow and it was warm enough to sit outside in the sun. "Looks as though we **drew the short straw**," said Alex and smiled at me with one eye. The other was hidden behind a black **patch**.

I nodded and smiled back like an idiot. What was he doing there? Shouldn't he be skiing with the others ...

"I thought I'd still be able to ski," he said as though he could read my mind, "but it's no good with one eye – you can't see the moguls." He dropped down into a deckchair beside me. "How's your thumb?"

"I'll live," I **squawked**. I was already drowning

---

to gasp – nach Luft schnappen; to pant – keuchen; exertion – Anstrengung; pro – Profi; fatal – tödlich; to draw the short straw – den Kürzeren ziehen; patch – Augenklappe; to squawk – krächzen

in the depths of his amazing right eye. It twinkled at me.

"What's that?" He nodded in the direction of the **sketchpad** in my lap.

"Just a few sketches," I said, feeling myself **blush**.

"**Mind** if I look?"

I'm good at art. That's another thing I **inherited** from Dad. He's a professional illustrator. He can draw your picture in a single **stroke**, and he never makes mistakes. Suddenly I was scared of showing my stuff to Alex. What if he thought it was crap?

"Go on, please ... " He looked **pleadingly** at me with one eye.

Fine. I showed him the sketchpad. The picture was called "Left foot on a balcony in the Alps". I chewed my lip nervously.

"But this is amazing!" said Alex in surprise. He studied the picture carefully. "Can you draw people, too? I mean, well enough to get the likeness?"

"Sure," I said.

"Can you draw me?"

"Sure," I said again. I was too much in love to think of anything more intelligent.

---

sketchpad – Zeichenblock; to blush – rot werden;
to mind – etwas dagegen haben; to inherit – erben;
stroke – Strich; pleading – flehend

Drawing someone allows you to stare at them for a very long time. You don't have to hide it. I took for ever, **lingering over** every little detail. Alex looked so cute with his dark curls peeking out from under his hat and his patch across his eye. He looked a bit like a pirate. He wouldn't stay still, though. Alex is really **fidgety**: he's always tapping his foot or fiddling with his earphones. He can't sit still for a minute. Maybe it's because his dad is a DJ and he's dancing to the beat. Or maybe it's because he has moved around so much. Alex and his mum have always lived wherever his dad gets a gig. They spent a few months in Goa (that's in India), then Ibiza, London and Berlin. It's enough to make anyone **fidget**. Alex had a thousand stories to tell and I listened to him admiringly. Then I told him about my weird family, about Benno, who can't live for a second without his Game Boy, about Mum, who's got a thing about helping people and is always collecting stuff – blankets for Romanians with rheumatism or **life buoys** for flood victims in Bangladesh – and Dad, who's always having great ideas.

"He keeps talking about the countryside, about going back to nature." I paused and gave a groan. I couldn't think of anything worse – except maybe

---

to linger over – sich Zeit lassen bei;
fidgety – hibbelig, zappelig; to fidget – zappeln;
life buoy – Rettungsboje

getting married to Fat Mario. "Thank God it won't happen."

"You can say that again. Villages are boring." Alex **twirled** his earphones.

I finished sketching and presented him with his portrait. Now it was my turn to tap my foot nervously and play with my pencil.

"Unbelievable." Alex **gazed** at the picture as though he was looking in the mirror. "It's amazing."

I felt myself go red again.

"Do you know what I'm going to do with it?" he asked. Apparently, his parents had been fighting on the day we left Munich, and his mum had **threatened** to get a divorce. That's why he'd been so **moody** in the gondola. His parents had made up again, but now he wanted to show them how he felt. He was going to tear the portrait in two and give them one half each. That way they'd only have all of him if they stayed together.

By the time he'd finished telling me, I was hopelessly in love.

"You're sooo sweet," I heard someone say softly. The voice sounded like mine. I glanced round in horror. Alex was the only other person there, so it must have been me. How embarrassing!

---

to twirl – herumwirbeln; to gaze – starren;
to threaten – drohen; moody – schlecht gelaunt

"You're pretty sweet, too, you know," said Alex and kissed me.

By the time Dad picked me up from the bus at the end of the holiday, I had a permanent grin on my face.

"Shame about the **injury**," said Dad, staring at me from the side, "but it looks like you enjoyed yourself."

"You could say that," I answered and didn't **bother** to explain. Why make a big deal of the fact that I had a boyfriend? I couldn't really believe it myself. The first kiss had lead to lots, lots more. Alex was totally sweet, and I was public enemy number one among the girls in my class.

Suse was pleased for me, though. If I was seeing Alex, maybe his dad would be able to pull some strings when Robbie came to town. Surely famous DJs could do that kind of thing.

Meanwhile, Dad was grinning to himself at the wheel. God knows why. Maybe he'd entered a prize draw with Greenpeace and won a week **chained** to the outside of an Arctic **oil-rig**, all **expenses** paid. Or maybe Mum had **donated** her **wilting** plants to blind **lepers** in West Tanzania

---

injury – Verletzung; to bother – sich die Mühe machen;
chained – angekettet; oil-rig – Ölplattform;
expenses – Ausgaben; to donate – schenken;
wilting – welkend; leper – Leprakranke/-r

and was paying her husband more attention at last. Or maybe Benno had got rid of his **evil** Game Boy and asked for an educational toy like a **mouth organ** instead.

"You seem to be enjoying yourself, too," I commented.

"You could say that," Dad **teased** me, grinning even more.

At that point I should have suspected something, but the alarm bells didn't go off. Even Mum's nervous blinking didn't warn me that something was wrong. I was still floating on a romantic cloud nine.

"There you are, love," she exclaimed when I walked into the kitchen. She stopped stirring a pan of **red cabbage** for long enough to give me a hug, then turned straight back to the stove. A **crispy pork roast** was sizzling in the oven.

When did she ever cook roasts? What was going on? I was getting a weird feeling. "Are we celebrating something?" I demanded, eyeing Mum **suspiciously**.

"Having you back," she said, her eye **twitching** frantically. She covered it with her hand.

I stopped to talk to Benno on the way to my

---

evil – böse; mouth organ – Mundharmonika;
to tease – necken; red cabbage – Rotkohl; crispy – knusprig; pork roast – Schweinebraten; suspicious – misstrauisch; to twitch – zucken

room. Maybe he'd know something. He's only nine and obsessed with his Game Boy, but he's not as **clueless** as you'd think. I found him playing computer games as usual, staring at the tiny screen with a look of determination on his face. "Big changes ahead," he **muttered**. "A new start for us all." He sounded like a mystic prophet from one of his favourite adventure games.

"Changes? What kind of changes?"

Benno **shrugged** and disappeared into the big wide world of computer-generated life.

When Mum called us for dinner, the table was laid festively with blue-and-white Bavarian serviettes. Why all the fuss? All of a sudden, I knew what we were celebrating. "Hey! I know what's up. You've been awarded the Bavarian **order of merit** for your charity work!"

"If only," growled Mum, dishing out **dumplings** onto our plates. "But most people don't appreciate that kind of thing."

By now her eye was opening and closing more frantically than ever, and her other eye was twitching, too. Dad seemed really excited. He carved the roast happily, grinning **mischievously** like a kid in the middle of a practical joke.

---

clueless – ahnungslos; to mutter – murmeln;
to shrug – mit den Schultern zucken; order of merit – Verdienstorden; dumpling – Kloß, Knödel;
mischievous – verschmitzt, schelmisch

"Spit it out, Dad," I said **grumpily**. "Let me guess: you've won the lottery. No, don't tell me, Mum's going to have a baby. Isn't it time you told us what's going on?"

"Enjoy your meal," Dad said cheerily.

"But Dad!"

"Put that thing away, Benno!" Mum **scolded** him. "I've told you a thousand times that Game Boys aren't allowed at the table."

"Come on, Dad, tell us!"

"Benno!"

I groaned and laid my head on the table. Then I noticed how Dad was looking questioningly at Mum. Her eyes were going crazy, but her head nodded briefly in encouragement. Time seemed to slow down as Dad took a long sip of beer. Then he took Mum's hand and looked at us both with shining eyes. "It's simple really," he said, taking his time over every syllable. "We're proud owners of a house!"

"**No kidding**?" At first I was just surprised – I hadn't seen that one coming.

"No kidding!" Dad **assured** me. "We bought it last week. A real **bargain**. We had to act fast."

Benno's hand reached out in the direction of his

---

grumpy – mürrisch; to scold – schimpfen;
No kidding? – Kein Witz?; to assure – versichern;
bargain – Schnäppchen

Game Boy. Before he could touch it, Mum grabbed it and dumped it on the shelf. How could he think of his stupid Game Boy at a time like this?

My head started to **steam**. My brain felt like an out of control **pinball machine**, with thousands of thoughts racing inside. A house! Was that a good thing? Hmm, maybe not ... Should I laugh or cry? After a while the thoughts clumped together into a single question – the **decisive** pinball, so to speak. "Where?"

Mum cleared her throat.

"In Lower Bavaria," answered Dad, rubbing his hands in excitement. "That's proper countryside for you."

"No!"

"Yes!"

The gigantic pinball exploded.

"Are you crazy???"

"We'll have much more room there," Dad said happily. "We'll have an **orchard**, we'll grow our own vegetables and we'll even have animals: ducks, chickens, dogs. Whatever you like! You always wanted pets!"

"Sure I did," I screamed at him. "When I was six! Now I'm 13 and I've got a boyfriend. I don't want any pets!"

---

to steam – dampfen; pinball machine – Flipper; decisive – entscheidend; orchard – Obstgarten

"You've got a boyfriend?" chorused both my parents together.

"Yes, as it happens. He's called Alex. It started last week."

"Well, we won't be a million miles away," said Dad. "Just wait till you see it!"

We may as well have been a million miles away. The house is in hell. Or in Höllenhausen, at least. Höllenhausen is the name of a collection of houses that calls itself a village. Legend has it that the devil came to earth there and **seduced** a young **maiden**. If you ask me, an **evil spirit** was there last week and got into my father. I can't see any other explanation for buying a **decrepit** old farm.

It was raining the next day when we went there. It took nearly 24 hours to get there from Munich because the countryside is full of tractors dropping **crap** on the road. My **mood** was in a downward spiral and it hit rock bottom when we finally reached the dream house. I got out of the car and **trod** in a juicy **cowpat**.

"I'll stay here," said Benno, switching on his Game Boy.

"No you won't," said Mum, **dragging** him into

---

to seduce – verführen; maiden – Jungfrau;
evil spirit – böser Geist; decrepit – altersschwach;
crap – Mist; mood – Laune; to trod – treten;
cowpat – Kuhfladen; to drag – schleifen, zerren

the rain. Benno's Game Boy was one of the reasons Mum and Dad had wanted to move in the first place. They wanted their son to stop playing video games and start climbing trees outside.

I scraped most of the cowpat off my shoe and took a look at the farmyard. The farm was at the edge of the village, as though the other houses wanted nothing to do with it. I couldn't blame them.

"Sure, we'll need to do some renovating, but it doesn't take much imagination to see what a jewel we've bought for ourselves." Dad looked at me expectantly.

"*You've* bought for *yourselves,*" I **hissed** back at him. After that I kept quiet and went on strike. There was no way I wanted to speak to **selfish** guys like these. They thought they were caring parents, yeah, right! They could put up with my silence until they sold their crappy farm.

OK, which flowerpot goes first? Maybe I'll start with Mum's beloved marguerites. She appears on the balcony and I cross my arms quickly. Throw a flowerpot? Who, me? I'd never do a thing like that.

"What are you up to, darling?" Mum starts picking off the dead leaves with a satisfied expression on her face. She'll probably start **humming** soon.

---

to hiss – zischen; selfish – egoistisch;
to hum – summen

"Me? I'm … I … Can I have those … marguerites?"

Mum looks at me, **frowning**. She doesn't like the idea of taking two living plants from their natural habitat – a flowerpot seven storeys above the main road. How will they survive?

"They're for Suse and Alex," I say. "To remember me by." That was **neat**.

Mum cuts off two flowers, hands them to me and looks me in the eye. "Come on, Annika, it's important to embrace new experiences."

"Is it?"

I head off with my two marguerites.

"Isn't it time you started packing?" Mum calls after me.

"Later."

I disappear. I'm supposed to be meeting Suse and Alex at the Olympic Tower. It was their idea. God knows what they're planning. It's cold and misty outside. I pull my scarf round my neck and make for the underground. Four lanes of traffic have come to a standstill. I take a deep breath as though I'm filling my lungs with sea air. The sweet smell of pollution! Not to mention the magical music of drivers sounding their horns … I love the smell of the city, the noisiness, the

---

to frown – die Stirn runzeln;
neat – *hier:* schnippisch, frech

crowds. I don't even mind when people **elbow** me – in Höllenhausen I'll be sharing the pavement with cows.

Suse had been shocked when she first heard about the catastrophe. I'd gone straight to her place and we'd cried our eyes out. We've been friends since our first day at school. Her parents weren't divorced back then – that's how long ago it was.

"We can't let them move," she kept saying. "We'll find a way."

We came up with all kinds of different action plans. We could go on hunger strike, refuse to talk, sit down and never get up. Suse wanted to start a petition protesting against my "forced deportation to the countryside". If all else **failed**, we could run away with Alex to London: Suse would introduce herself to Robbie, and he'd invite us to live at his **mansion**. In the end, we had to **shelve the plan**: it wouldn't be fair on Suse's mum. It wouldn't have worked anyway. Refusing to speak didn't help much either – it just put us all in a bad mood.

I take the escalator to the station. A **gust** of stuffy air comes towards me. Ah, the lovely station air! A punk asks for money. **Begging** usually annoys me, but I give him 50 cents.

---

to elbow – anrempeln; to fail – schiefgehen;
mansion – Villa; to shelve a plan – einen Plan verwerfen;
gust – Windstoß; to beg – betteln

Alex didn't cry when I told him. He's a **laid-back** kind of guy. He knows what it's like to move. It has happened to him **loads of times**. "Crying won't help," he told me and acted like nothing had happened. We hung out, went skating, listened to music, kissed, danced, played basketball, kissed, kissed and kissed, as though I didn't have to move away. Life's never boring with Alex – he's always on the go.

He can't pretend it's not happening now, though. The Easter holidays start tomorrow. Suse and her mum will be driving to her grandma's, and Alex and his parents are flying to Ibiza. When they're back, I'll be gone.

I stride towards the television tower and spot the two of them from a distance: my best friend and my boyfriend.

"Hi," says Alex with a winning smile, and kisses me.

"Hi," I say and take the elevator with them to the top of the highest tower in Munich. The wind blows around our heads as we stand on the viewing platform. I gaze down at the city, my city, and a **lump** comes to my throat.

"We had an idea," says Suse, pointing into the distance. "Look, you'll be living over there."

---

laid-back – cool; loads of times – viele Male;
lump – Kloß

I turn to look, but there's nothing but **mist**.

"Every Monday Alex and I will come up here at three. We'll look this way and think of you. If you do the same, it'll feel like we're together."

I start to cry.

---

mist – Nebel

Update from the Village Front

Countryside correspondent Annika Weber with all the latest news ...

This is Annika Weber reporting from the Weber household's "jewel", an old farmhouse dating back to the **previous** century. It's a remarkable place. Mr and Mrs Weber were lucky to get it. The building is practically antique. As a professional journalist it's important that I'm objective, but sometimes it's tricky. Really tricky.

The Bavarian countryside is going through an unusually wet period. To put it another way, **it's raining cats and dogs**. In fact, it's even raining in Annika Weber's oh-so **spacious** new bedroom, which is why she's moved to the **larder** instead.

"The roof won't take long to fix," Mr Weber said **breezily**. "It's just a teeny little hole." The builders can't start work for another eight weeks.

Unfortunately for the Webers, the teeny little hole is actually one of many. Thanks to the 20 or

---

previous – vergangen, vorig;
It's raining cats and dogs. – Es regnet wie aus Kübeln.;
spacious – geräumig; larder – Speisekammer;
breezy – kess

so **leaks** in the roof, the entire upper floor of the house is now uninhabitable. All four members of the Weber household are living in **cramped** conditions on the ground floor.

"Your dad will have to fix the roof himself!" Mrs Weber declared, turning her attention to the kitchen. She was determined to give the place a good clean and **reveal** the beautiful parquet flooring. So far no one knows what lies **beneath** the dirt. Mrs Weber couldn't start cleaning because the **taps** won't work.

"Who needs tap water anyway?" her daughter joked. "We've got plenty of rain water. Let's buy a couple of buckets and catch the drips from the roof."

"I'll phone the water board and ask them to turn on the **supply**," said Mr Weber. Sadly, that wasn't the problem. The village **plumbers** are fully booked until June.

Thankfully, the Webers can make use of a charming **outhouse**, complete with a bucket. Farmers in the 19th century used the arrangement to satisfy their toilet needs. The waste products land in a bucket, thus avoiding the need for a **flush**. That's

---

leak – Loch, Leck; cramped – beengt;
to reveal – zum Vorschein bringen; beneath – unter;
tap – Wasserhahn; supply – Versorgung;
plumber – Installateur; outhouse – *hier:* Plumpsklo;
flush – Spülung

the up-side. The down-side is the unusual **lack of** anything resembling a **drain**. The bucket has to be emptied every second day. Worse still, the outhouse – a wooden structure with a heart carved into its door – is located in the open air. Miles away from anywhere, and nowhere near the house.

"What if it's dark, the **owls** are hooting, and it's pouring with rain?" asked Annika Weber in horror.

"You'll have to wear your gum boots," Mr Weber said firmly. "It won't be for ever, you know."

The decision was taken to set up a chicken **pen** to stop Hannchen, Helga and Hermann escaping. (If you ask me, that would **suit** everyone, but my opinion doesn't count.)

No one realized that Hermann's body clock is several hours fast (probably the result of a war injury) and he always **crows** at 04.00. He's as reliable as **clockwork**.

During their first night in the village none of the Webers closed any of their collective eight eyes. Mr Weber was worrying about how to get the water to work, and Mrs Weber was planning her organic vegetable patch. Meanwhile, Annika Weber was convinced that **a host of** toothless ghosts would **emerge** from the cellar and take their revenge for

---

lack of – Mangel an; drain – Abflussrohr; owl – Eule;
pen – Gehege; to suit – passen; to crow – krähen;
clockwork – Uhrwerk; a host of – jede Menge;
to emerge – auftauchen, hervorkommen

a lifetime spent in Höllenhausen (never **underestimate** the anger of a village ghost!). Benno Weber, on the other hand, took advantage of the situation and stayed up all night with his Game Boy. He's now on level 10.

At 04.15 Hermann finished his **nocturnal** concert, and everyone got up.

"If we're going to get up this early, we may as well buy a cow. Then at least we'll have fresh milk," said Mrs Weber. Her daughter didn't answer: she was cleaning her teeth over a **puddle**.

At the end of the first week the household included two chickens, one **cockerel**, a cow, two cats, a dog and a **guinea pig**. The guinea pig had been bought at Benno Weber's request. He kept it in a cage in a darkened **broom** cupboard.

"Why not get an animal that can run around outside?" his mother had suggested.

"You mean **cooped up** in a pen like Hannchen, Helga and Hermann? No thanks!" her son replied.

The guinea pig was named Guinea Pig.

Halfway through the week Mr and Mrs Weber decided to get to know their neighbours. "It's important to be part of the **community**."

---

to underestimate – unterschätzen; nocturnal – nächtlich; puddle – Pfütze; cockerel – Hahn; guinea pig – Meerschweinchen; broom – Besen; cooped up – eingesperrt; community – Gemeinde, Gemeinschaft

Mr and Mrs Weber **strode** through the village, **beaming at** the passers-by. Their daughter grimaced: being part of the community wasn't one of her priorities. Benno Weber looked miserable. He'd been forced to part with his Game Boy.

"Try to smile a bit, Annika. What will people think?"

"That's their business."

The **mayor** served beer. He beamed back at the Webers and welcomed Mr Weber into the village **rifle club**. "The women," he told Mrs Weber, "bake cakes for the **annual** village fête."

Mr and Mrs Weber stopped smiling and their daughter grinned instead. Mr Weber rejected his rifle club membership on ideological grounds. "As a youngster, I was a **conscientious objector**," he explained. Now the mayor stopped smiling, too. The beer warmed up, the mood turned frosty, and the village builders had busier **schedules** than before. They won't start work until Christmas.

The Webers took their leave, fetched their dog and wandered round the village without knocking on any more doors. Mr and Mrs Weber started a technical discussion about whether the rifle club

---

to stride – schreiten; to beam at sb – jmdn. anstrahlen;
mayor – Bürgermeister; rifle club – Schützenverein;
annual – jährlich;
conscientious objector – Wehrdienstverweigerer;
schedule – Terminplan

had anything to do with war. The matter was never resolved because the dog ran away and everyone had to search for it until nightfall. After a while Annika Weber **volunteered to** empty the bucket in the outhouse. It had just begun to rain.

To sum up, the Easter holidays came and went, but the Webers' problems refused to go away. In fact, they're getting bigger by the day. **DIY** is not Mr Weber's strong point – he's totally and **utterly** useless. A friend drove down from the city to lend a hand, but broke his arm by falling off the roof. (It pains me to say it, but he was even more useless than Mr Weber himself.) Mrs Weber doesn't know how to milk, so it takes her all day. Meanwhile, her daughter chats on the phone to her best friend and her boyfriend, and her son plays on his Game Boy. All four Webers use the bucket in the outhouse, and Hermann crows at four – at 04.00 precisely.

School starts tomorrow, but it's a million miles away and only accessible by bus. The bus goes from village to village, collecting all the kids. It takes for ever. Annika and Benno Weber are the first to get on, so the journey takes an hour longer.

You've been listening to Annika Weber, live from the countryside at the heart of the action.

---

to volunteer to do sth – etwas freiwillig tun;
DIY (Do It Yourself) – Heimwerken; utterly – völlig, total

Ta Da!

It's first thing in the morning, it's **misty** outside, and Benno and I are waiting for the bus.

"I can't believe it," I hiss to myself. I'm standing in the fog at seven in the morning, it's not even light yet, and the air smells of dung. It wouldn't surprise me if a herd of monster cows emerged from the mist. They'd come towards us without warning – no bells, just the **occasional snort** – and cover us in cowpats. Instead the bus comes along.

I woke up in the larder this morning. I'll be sleeping there until the roof is fixed in several **decades** time. It's **musty** and dark, with just a single tiny window right up near the ceiling. The glass has never been cleaned because people don't **tend to** need windows in their larders. The good thing is the storage space – I can put my stuff on countless shelves covered in **gherkin mould** and jam **stains**. What more could I want?

---

misty – neblig; occasional – gelegentlich;
snort – Schnauben; decade – Jahrzehnt; musty – muffig;
to tend to – neigen zu; gherkin – Essiggurke;
mould – Schimmel; stain – Fleck

Hermann maintained a two-week tradition by waking us up at four. There's nothing I like better than walking across the yard to the outhouse in the dark. I'm a fan of darkness, whatever the situation. My **extensive** knowledge of crime novels and horror films means I know exactly what's **lurking** out of sight in the shadows. Now I'm suffering from lack of sleep, and I fall over my feet as I get on the bus.

"Careful, young lady. You'd better look where you're going," says the bus driver. His face looks yellow from too many cigarettes. He's **skinny** as a **rake** – probably because he can't find a wife who'll put up with the smoking. And his nicotine **addiction** seems to make him moody, too.

"I'm Joe, the bus driver. No latecomers, no chocolate marks on the seats and no screaming. Those are the rules, and you'll damn well stick to them."

Who the hell does he think he is? Benno pays no attention – he's busy with his Game Boy and walks past in silence. Mum and Dad's computer cure hasn't exactly worked. I'm not even sure Benno could identify a tree, let alone climb one.

"How about a 'Good Morning'?" growls Joe.

---

extensive – umfassend; to lurk – lauern; skinny – dünn; rake – Harke; addiction – Abhängigkeit

"Wasn't in the rules," mutters Benno, **plonking** himself **down** by the window.

I sit next to him and stare at my **sneakers**. There's a heart on one of them (Alex) and an 'A' for anarchy (Suse) to remind me that I mustn't let **a bunch of** village kids tell me what to do. I chat to Suse on the phone every day.

Another couple of kids get in. The girl looks about my age, and her brother is probably in the same class as Benno. They're wearing **checked** shirts (!) **tucked** into stonewashed jeans (!!).

"Good morning, Joe!"

"Good morning, Mona, good morning, Christian!"

Joe directs a triumphant glance at Benno. *Look at these two,* he's telling him, *they know how to behave*. Benno hasn't seen or heard anything. It's no use trying to get through to him.

Christian goes to the back of the bus, but Mona sits across the **aisle** from me. She puts down her school bag – an old leather **satchel** that she probably inherited from her dad. She turns to me. "If there's anything you need, that's our house over there."

Mona lives in our village but on the other side.

---

to plonk oneself down – sich hinschmeißen;
sneaker – Turnschuh; a bunch of – ein paar;
checked – kariert; to tuck – stecken; aisle – Gang;
satchel – Ranzen

Her family owns an enormous farm on the top of a hill without a proper road – I guess cows prefer to walk on mud.

I can't imagine I'll ever need anything from her, but I **nod** and try to smile.

The bus stops every few metres and soon it's pretty crowded. The others are staring at us. They're not even trying to hide their curiosity. Well, let them stare – I'm from Munich where there's life and love. I'll show them. I'll **stir** things **up** and kick them out of their lethargy, out of their sleepy village ways. Ta da! The city girl's here to teach the farmers how to live!

Joe stops outside the school, and I wait until last to get off. I don't want any village kids staring at my **bum**. My **butt** belongs to the city! The kids **surge** towards a low white building. At my old school it would have been covered in graffiti, but here it's sparkling white. Everyone knows each other and they're chatting about the holidays. I bet they haven't got anything interesting to say. The biggest **thrill** was probably stealing sweets from the corner shop or something.

Benno **traipses** into the building, eyes fixed on his Game Boy. **Beats me** how he manages to walk

---

to nod – nicken; to stir up – wachrütteln;
bum/butt – Hintern; to surge – strömen;
thrill – Nervenkitzel; to traipse – latschen;
Beats me ... – *hier:* Ich frage mich ...

through the doors, go forwards without bumping into stuff and find his way to the classroom. At one o'clock he'll traipse back out again, eyes still fixed on his Game Boy, and everything will be OK.

All of a sudden, I'm the only one left. For a moment I think about hanging around outside until Joe turns up to drive us home. I could always call Alex to tell him that I miss him. But Alex is at school – our school. I guess I can't wait around for ever, so I may as well go inside.

The Latin teacher is waiting at the door. What a perfect way to start the day. I bet he'll want to introduce me to the class, and I'll have to put up with them staring again – staring and staring until their eyes pop out of their heads.

His name is Schmidt-Bürste. "Schmidt by birth and Bürste because of my wife," he says with a grin.

Oh God. A 21st-century Latin teacher. A Latin teacher who smiles. You don't get that in the city.

I follow Schmidt-Bürste into the classroom. The class gets up. "Good morning, sir!"

It reminds me of primary school. I laugh out loud.

Schmidt-Bürste smiles. "Plonk yourself down anywhere."

What a cool guy.

"Oh, Annika, one more thing: remember to bring your slippers tomorrow." He points at the carpet.

I laugh again. What a funny guy. Then I look down: 25 pairs of farmers' feet in 25 pairs of glamorous slippers. He has to be kidding. I'm not going to wear slippers. I don't even possess a pair.

Schmidt-Bürste **gestures to** an empty desk. "Why don't you sit there?"

I look at his scruffy leather shoes. Leather shoes and cord trousers.

"How come you're not wearing slippers then?" I ask.

The village kids start whispering and giggling. I stare Schmidt-Bürste in the eye. I want an answer. If I have to wear slippers, so should he. I'm not posting a pair of slippers to Munich for Alex and Suse to **embroider** their names. I won't be parted from my sneakers!

Schmidt-Bürste removes his cord jacket and hangs it on the back of his chair. He sits down and smiles at me. His shirt is made of cord – well, no surprises there. "Only the pupils wear slippers here."

I'm practically speechless. What kind of answer is that?

"Now sit down please, Annika."

For the time being the discussion is closed. I sit at my desk. Schmidt-Bürste might not want to talk

---

to gesture to – deuten auf;
to embroider – sticken

about it, but I've no intention of wearing slippers. No way!

The lesson goes as expected – Latin is Latin, I guess. Schmidt-Bürste tries to get his revenge by asking lots of questions, but he can't catch me out.

I look round the room. The village kids look quite normal really. Only Mona looks like a farmer's daughter. There's a **spare** place at her desk, and I thank God that Schmidt-Bürste didn't make me sit there. Having my own desk suits me fine. While we're waiting for our Maths teacher, I take the opportunity to write *ALEX* in big letters on my desk.

"Annika? Hi, I'm Jockel. I liked the way you stood up to Schmidt-Bürste. We should start a **petition**."

I look at the guy standing in front of me. Sun shines through his **protruding** ears, and his small round glasses are so dirty that I can't see the colour of his eyes. He turns to the class. "Hey, who's up for starting a petition?"

Everyone laughs and shakes their head. Idiot.

Jockel shrugs and grins. "Seriously, Annika, I'd put my name down."

An idiot, but kind of sweet all the same.

---

spare – frei; petition – Unterschriftensammlung; protruding – abstehend

At break-time they all go outside. Slippers off, shoes on. I wait in the corridor by the window.

"*Everyone* goes outside at break-time," Mona tells me. Her shirt is still tucked into her jeans.

Sure, but why would I listen to anyone in slippers?! I stay right where I am, take a seat on the window **ledge** and start drawing in my sketchpad: "Village Kids at Play." The view from the second-floor window reminds me of my old school. People chatting, kicking cans, **French skipping** – a general mass of moving kids. But Alex isn't here and my heart belongs to him. My parents can move wherever they like – Alex and I belong together.

"I'll never forget you," Alex told me. I was worried he might break up with me because I'd lost my city cool. I'm not scared now, though. The two of us will make it together.

"Mmm, not bad!"

I whirl round in surprise. I hadn't realized anyone was watching me. I turn the page quickly, even though he's already seen it. It's none of his business. Why isn't he outside with the others?

"Don't suppose you'd be interested in helping, would you?"

He's a good-looking guy, really good-looking. For a village kid he's seriously attractive. **Messy**

---

ledge – Sims; French skipping – Gummitwist; messy – wirr

blond hair and a laid-back look. His jeans are covered in paint. He might not be a pupil; he might be **apprenticed** to a painter. I bet he works for a decorating firm in Munich and has been brought in because the village **labourers** are booked out for the next few years. But that doesn't explain why he wants me to help him …

"I'm in charge of the **set** for the drama club's musical. It's a big job for one person. I'll never make the deadline on my own."

He stares at me with his bright green eyes. I can't look into them for long.

"Anyway, we'll be in the drama room at one, if you're interested."

He walks off. He's probably heading outside. He turns round one last time. "Nice sketch."

I stare at the **revolving door** until it stops moving and the silence of slippered feet returns. He'd better not think he can talk me into helping him. *I'm* the one who decides what I do.

The **rehearsal** has started by the time I find the drama room. I recognize the music straight away: it's my favourite musical, The Rocky Horror Picture Show. It's been showing at a cinema in Mu-

---

to be apprenticed – in der Ausbildung sein;
labourer – *hier:* Handwerker; set – Bühnenbild, Kulisse;
revolving door – Schwingtür; rehearsal – Probe

nich for the past century or so. I've seen it at least five times with Suse.

Somehow it seems fitting. It's about a couple, Brad and Janet, who get lost in the rain. They find an old house in the middle of nowhere, knock on the door and are trapped in a **nightmare**.

I know how it feels.

It's dark inside. Brad and Janet, played by a couple of village kids, are standing in the spot lights, while a troupe of dancers do the "Time Warp" in the background. The movie is much better, of course, but for a bunch of amateurs they're not too bad. I **hover** in the doorway and decide not to stay. Instead, I find myself walking in. Janet sings really well, brilliantly actually. With a bit of effort they could really pull this off. I look at the half-finished set. It's the inside of an old house – nothing too complicated. I could design it in my sleep. They've got to the part where Dr Frank N. Furter bursts out of an elevator. In this production he pops up from behind a **cardboard** wall. It doesn't really work.

"You should make the door of **cloth**, so he can push his way out. And you need to show the movement of the elevator. Why not use lights or something?"

---

nightmare – Albtraum; to hover – herumstehen; cardboard – Pappe; cloth – Stoff

Damn. I need to learn to keep my mouth shut.

Everyone turns and **squints**. They can't see me in the darkness.

The rehearsal comes to a halt.

"Who said that?" the drama teacher asks.

"I did." I couldn't exactly **deny** it.

"And who are you?"

"Annika ... the new girl from Munich."

The actors exchange glances and the teacher frowns. There's a mood of **disapproval**.

"Well, sorry, Annika, but the set is Georg's business, and I'm not sure you ..."

Georg. The guy with the beautiful eyes.

"OK, forget it. I'm just talking crap."

Let them say what they like, so long as I can go. Georg is blocking the door, though. "Great idea, Annika. Let's do it like that." He walks on to the stage. "Where shall we put the elevator?"

Georg wants my advice. He's asking me about the elevator. Hmm, the elevator ... "Well, it's centre-stage in the movie. It's a **crucial** moment. All eyes are on the elevator when Dr Frank N. Furter arrives in the room."

George stands in the middle of the stage. "Do you mean here?"

I look at him, then the others.

---

to squint – blinzeln; to deny – leugnen;
disapproval – Missbilligung; crucial – entscheidend

They stare back. *Say something, Annika! Say anything at all!*

"Um, yes," I squawk.

Mum picks me up in the car. Joe and the school bus left ages ago.

"I'm so proud of you, Annika! Making friends on your very first day. Which character are you playing?"

Making friends?? Who said I'd made friends? "I'm not acting, Mum. I'm helping with the set."

"Well, that's wonderful, darling. Just your thing. So what are they like then?"

No comment.

I fasten my seatbelt. Mum's driving too fast again. She glances over, waiting for me to say that I love my new school.

"Oh, come on, Annika. It can't be that bad!"

Still no comment.

"Your dad bought a toilet today. He got it half-price."

Ever since my parents bought their "jewel", we've had to get everything half-price. We can't even afford a proper toilet! I check the time: 14.30. In half an hour I need to be at the top of the hill where Mona milks her cows. Mum is still going on about how lovely it is here. According to her, we're really lucky to have a house without water – not everyone knows that water doesn't come straight from a tap. Living without warmth and **creature comforts** is a valuable experience ... Oh, and Helga has laid her first egg. Mum asks me to have a word with Benno. "He's still obsessed with his Game Boy. Why don't you talk to him? Tell him how great it is here."

We're home now, so I grab the dog and head out.

Mum wanted me to have the dog. "You need to think of a name for him. If you don't call him something, he'll never **obey** you."

Why can't she just leave me alone? It's not my fault she keeps having these ideas. I'm *not* going to have a word with Benno, and a dog is just a dog. I didn't decide to live here – they did.

There's a tree and a bench at the top of the hill. I'll come here every Monday. It doesn't matter if I sit down because I can't see Munich anyway. I know which way the tower is, and that's what really counts.

The dog must have smelled something because he's **digging** under the bench. Three o'clock exactly. Hi Alex! Hi Suse! How I'd love to be with them in Munich. I close my eyes and send my thoughts and feelings over the hill, along the motorway and up to the top of the tower. I see the two

---

creature comfort – leibliches Wohl;
to obey – gehorchen; to dig – graben

of them on the viewing platform, hands in their pockets, wind blowing round their heads, sending their thoughts and feelings across the fields to me. If a plane mysteriously crashes, we'll know why: our thoughts and feelings met in the sky and **fused** in a cloud of togetherness.

The dog jumps up. He's covered from head to **toe** in mud – and now the same goes for me. I grab his front **paws** and look into his eyes. "What's your name?"

The dog looks back. *Georg*. The name pops into my mind. Maybe the dog is called Georg. How the hell did I come up with that? The dog's got beautiful eyes, a messy **coat** and **mud-spattered** fur like the paint on Georg's trousers. But what would Alex think if I called my dog after someone else? Bad idea.

"OK, tell me your name then."

The dog pulls away, rolls in the mud and shows me his muddy **belly**. ***Stroke** me!* There's no mistaking that **command**.

I bend down and **tickle** him. "Come one, tell me your name!"

The dog lies on his back, **wagging his tail**.

---

to fuse – verschmelzen; toe – Zehe; paw – Pfote;
coat – *hier:* Fell; mud-spattered – mit Matsch bespritzt;
fur – Fell; belly – Bauch; to stroke – streicheln;
command – Befehl; to tickle – *hier:* kraulen;
to wag his tail – mit dem Schwanz wedeln

“Rocky! That’s it! Rocky from the Rocky Horror Picture Show.”

Rocky jumps up and races around like a mad thing, running backwards and forwards, up and down. I guess he likes his new name.

Ute and Pute

"I miss you!"

"I miss you, too. Mario had a party on Saturday, and it was rubbish without you."

Mario's parties are always *amazing*. For one thing, his parents want everyone to be as fat as him, so there's always masses of food. Besides, Mario's house has a basement and no one complains if the music gets too loud. We can stay up as long as we like. Mario's parties are never boring. I swallow. This time I wasn't there.

"Tell me what happened then!"

"Have a guess."

"Don't say someone kissed Mario!"

Alex laughs his **cute** laugh. I can picture him exactly. He's smiling and doing a million things at once: using a bit of paper to clean his teeth, surfing the net, downloading MP3s, pulling his socks on and off, fidgeting on his seat …

I'm not doing anything except talking to him. Evening sunlight **pours** through my tiny window

---

cute – süß; to pour – strömen

and Rocky snores at my feet. I cleaned the window myself. It was one hell of a job and it would have been quicker to buy some new glass. The **glaziers** are too busy to fit it, though.

"No way! No, Ute and Pute swapped around."

"Ute's going out with Sascha?"

"Exactly. And Pute's seeing Ute! Hang on, I mean Pute's seeing Lukas."

I can't help wondering about Alex. He's dating a village kid. Maybe I shouldn't ask too many questions. What if he says, "Er, Annika, I've got a **confession** to make ..." or "I've got two girlfriends: one from the country and one from the city. Do you know Biggi with the enormous breasts?"?

"Sounds like a good party. What did Suse get up to?"

Alex laughs. There's as much chance of Suse getting a boyfriend as someone kissing Mario. She isn't fat or ugly or anything, but her heart is set on Robbie Williams, and he wasn't there. "Suse DJ-ed. You can guess which album she played ..."

No surprises there.

"Hey, Annika, I'm sorry. I didn't mean to go on about the party." He dropped his voice to a whisper, "It was rubbish without you anyway."

Alex loves Annika the village kid – or at least it sounds as if he does. And he thinks the country-

---

glazier – Glaser; confession – Geständnis

side is boring: just empty space, village peace and morning mists …

"I guess you don't have parties in the middle of nowhere. What did you get up to on Saturday?"

Of course, they have parties here. OK, not this weekend, but we … I mean … *they* … well, of course, they have parties. I was too busy for a party on Saturday anyway. I spent the whole day working on the set. It's much harder than I expected. Sure, I'm used to sketching stuff on paper, but painting huge **canvases** is a completely different matter. Georg is really good at it. I love watching him paint. OK, maybe *love* is a bit **excessive**, but I could watch him for hours. He paints as though the colours were part of him, as though he didn't need the paint-pot or the brush at all. He doesn't care if he gets covered in paint or runs out of brown or whatever. He just mixes the colours himself. He knows which shade of brown he wants and he knows how to make it: a bit of this, a little of that, and **hey presto** – he gets the colour he was looking for.

Georg forgets about everything else when he's painting. He's even quieter than usual, just completely wrapped up in his work. He's not like other

---

canvas – Leinwand; excessive – übertrieben;
hey presto – plötzlich

guys – more **unapproachable**. I don't think he's interested in anything **but** his painting. Sometimes he looks up while I'm watching him and stares at me with his **fabulous** eyes, and I turn away quickly. I get on with my painting, and he gets on with his. We worked for hours **on end** on Saturday, then suddenly it was dark. I couldn't believe it. It's weird how time disappears like that. It would drive Alex crazy – he's far too fidgety to stand still.

Now and then Georg would get up and disappear down the corridor to buy a hot chocolate. He always came back empty-handed because you need the right change for the machine. Most **artists** are impractical, I guess.

I lend him the money if I've got it. He reappears a few minutes later, sipping his hot chocolate and looking at my work. I hear him blowing into his cup and I try not to say anything. I don't want to disappoint him. I want him to be pleased with my work.

"Good," he says usually, or even "excellent" sometimes. So far he's only had to help me once. On Wednesday I was supposed to be painting a **fiendish** dog. Georg asked my **permission**, handed me his chocolate, then added the finishing

---

unapproachable – unnahbar; but – *hier:* außer;
fabulous – sagenhaft; on end – ohne Unterbrechung;
artist – Künstler; fiendish – teuflisch;
permission – Erlaubnis

touches. Suddenly my harmless **canine** stopped looking like Rocky and became a hound of hell.

"You make it look so easy," I said admiringly.

Georg brushed aside my compliment. "I read loads of scary comics in my youth." He handed me my paintbrush and I gave him his cup.

"Are you into horror stories?"

Georg nodded. "I'm reading *Frankenstein* at the moment. I've read it hundreds of times before, but it's such a cool book."

"I prefer *Dracula,*" I said. "It sends shivers down my **spine**."

I often have visions of **Count** Dracula sailing in his **coffin** to London. At night he gets out and sinks his teeth into sailors. It makes my hair stand on end.

Georg said he hadn't read *Dracula*. Well, I could not allow that – *Dracula* is simply a *must*. I took my copy to school with me on Thursday and was about to go looking for him when he turned up in my classroom. "Are you busy on Saturday?" he asked in a business-like way. "I'm worried about the set. We've still got heaps to do."

"Saturday's fine by me," I said. I pulled out the book and gave it to him. "Here, read this. It'll scare you to death."

---

canine – Hündchen; spine – *hier:* Rücken;
count – Graf; coffin – Sarg

His green eyes **lit up** for a second. "Thanks, Annika!" The next moment he was gone.

"Where's *my* book?" Jockel stretched his hands out like a beggar and pretended to be **offended**.

Jockel is my right-hand man in the slipper resistance. He **swapped** desks so we could sit next to each other, and for a village kid and a city girl we make a good team. He's started wearing sneakers as well. We're walking, talking protesters – the demonstrating duo.

At the end of my first week Schmidt-Bürste lost his patience: "Annika, I know it's not easy changing schools but surely you can make an effort to stick to the rules."

That was Jockel's **cue**. He jumped up and pointed to his shoes. "Look, sir, I'm not wearing slippers either!"

Our teacher **sighed** and threatened to deal with us another day.

Anyway, back to *Dracula*. I told Jockel that he was too young to read horror stories. He **pulled a face** at me. "Speaking of horror stories," he said, chewing on a mouthful of **jelly babies**, "what about my slippers? We need to mobilize the crowds."

---

to light up – aufleuchten; offended – beleidigt;
to swap – tauschen; cue – Stichwort; to sigh – seufzen;
to pull a face – das Gesicht verziehen;
jelly baby – Gummibärchen

"I've got a better idea," I said, grabbing the sweets from his hand. "You could always try a hunger-strike!" Suddenly I felt a gust of cold air from behind me. Mona was glaring at me with ice-cold **hatred**.

"Shut up about your stupid slippers," she snapped.

Mona is weird. On the first day she offered to help me, but by the second day she was treating me like dirt. I even made an effort to smile at her, which was nice of me really, but she glared at me angrily. Her ice-cold eyes would have cut me in two if I hadn't ducked. Since then she's been frosty towards me, and I can't think why. I haven't done anything. I could understand if I'd told her that stonewashed jeans, **leather belts** and checked shirts are totally out, but I didn't say a word. I didn't even mention her hair, which she evidently cuts herself. I guess she doesn't realize that there's a long **straggly strand** hanging down her back. (OK, I know she leaves it there **on purpose** – in the countryside her hairstyle probably counts as cool.) I haven't said a word against her, and she still **hates my guts**.

"We all wear slippers," she hissed at me. "You're

---

hatred – Hass; leather belt – Ledergürtel;
straggly – unordentlich; strand – Strähne;
on purpose – absichtlich;
to hate sb's guts – jmdn. nicht ausstehen können

just a **stuck-up** city girl! No one cares what you think. If you don't like it, you should leave."

My mouth fell open in amazement. Mona hated me with a **passion**.

"Hey, Mona, that's not fair. I'm not wearing slippers either!" Jockel obviously felt left out. Mona ignored his attempt to stick up for me.

"Well?"

I **regained** control of my mouth. "For your information, I hate your crappy Höllenhausen. I hate catching the bus with Banana Joe. I hate living in a boring village. You can tell the devil's been there – he **poisoned** the minds of idiots like you."

Mona stared at me. She would have strangled me if our Maths teacher hadn't walked into the classroom. My life was **spared**, but she hadn't forgiven me, as I soon found out ...

That weekend, the same day as Mario's party, I'd been working in the drama room with Georg. We'd just finished building a horror shelf in the corner of the stage. Thick **drips** of **plaster** fell like heavy drops of blood from the wood. Georg was even quieter than usual, but he offered me a **lift** on his moped – God knows why I deserved such an

---

stuck-up – arrogant; passion – Leidenschaft;
to regain – wiedererlangen; to poison – vergiften;
to be spared – verschont bleiben; drip – Tropfen;
plaster – Putz; lift – Mitfahrgelegenheit

honour. We **spluttered along** for ages, past fields, **meadows** and cows. I had to keep my legs up the whole time and it hurt like hell, but it was actually kind of fun. I'd never ridden on a moped before and I liked the fact that Georg was no longer quite so unapproachable. Not that I'm interested in him, of course. But it was nice all the same ...

"Have you seen the devil's rocks?" he asked when we got to my house.

"The devil's rocks?"

"You know, where the devil seduced the maiden. You must have heard the legend!"

"Sure," I said.

"It's pretty spooky. I'll show you where it happened if you like."

"What, now?" I ask. Georg nodded.

I was about to get back on the moped when Mum appeared at the door and sent Benno out to play. "If you insist on playing on your stupid Game Boy, then at least go outside!"

"Blah blah blah," muttered Benno.

"Oh, there you are, Annika! Thank goodness you're back. You can **give** your father **a hand**." Mum disappeared inside the house.

"He should have thought of that before he bought this ruin," I moaned.

---

to splutter along – entlangtuckern; meadow – Wiese;
to give sb a hand – jmdm. helfen

Suddenly Benno reached up and planted a great big kiss on my cheek. I stared at him in astonishment. "It's from Alex," he explained. He traipsed into the garden, eyes fixed on his Game Boy.

"Maybe another time, then," said Georg.

I nodded. He lowered his **visor** and motored noisily away. I watched him go, then turned to walk into the house. I could feel someone staring at me. I looked back and saw Mona. She must have been watching all the time. She didn't move.

"What's your problem?" I yelled at her. "What are you staring at?"

Mona walked away silently.

"I don't get it!" I shouted. "Why don't you like me?"

"You're just another stupid city girl!" spat Mona, marching up the hill.

That was the Saturday when Ute and Pute swapped with Sascha and Lukas.

"I was partying on Saturday, too. I stayed up till four with Hermann in the outhouse."

Alex is silent for a moment. "With Hermann? Who ..."

I can't help laughing. "Hermann's a cockerel."

"You mean you **cheated on** me with a cockerel? How could you?"

---

visor – Visier; to cheat on sb – jmdn. betrügen

The door opens and Mum walks in. She's all dressed up because she's going to a **parish** meeting. The workmen and labourers will be there, which explains why Mum and Dad are keen to go. Her **cheeks** are flushed with excitement. She's probably hoping to persuade a builder, decorator or glazier to start work on our house. "We're off!" she **trills**.

I cover the mouthpiece with my hand and wave.

"Don't chat for too long. You know how much it costs!"

In Munich they never used to care how much things cost. Now every spare cent is swallowed by our "jewel". The door closes.

"I'm sorry, Alex, I have to go."

Alex sighs. "Already?"

I stare out of the little window into the dark night sky. "I can't wait to see you," I say softly. Why bother whispering? Alex won't get here any faster.

"I talked to Suse. We're saving all our pocket money."

Alex's parents don't have a car and Suse's mum is always working. They'll have to use public transport and that's a mission in itself: underground, train, another train, then the bus. Ugh.

---

parish – Gemeinde; cheek – Wange;
to trill – trillern, trällern

"It won't be long now, I promise."

Not long? How long is not long? I blow Alex a kiss through the phone line and he kisses me back. We hang up. I keep hold of the **handset** and listen to the beeps, trying to imagine him kissing me. Why do we forget that kind of stuff so quickly? It's not fair.

A storm is gathering outside. There's a crash as something **shatters** on the beautiful kitchen floor. I walk in and find Benno **rummaging** through the cupboards in desperation. "Do you know what they've done with it?" he asks.

Our parents have taken a stand: "If you're not smart enough to see the beauty of the countryside, we'll have to give you a helping hand." They took away his Game Boy.

It was a dumb thing to do. Benno hasn't stopped hunting for his Game Boy. He definitely hasn't had time to climb trees or anything. I feel a bit sorry for him but I don't know where it is.

"Maybe Mum planted it in the garden," I joke.

Benno isn't amused.

I make a sandwich, grab a biscuit for Rocky and go back to my room. The weather is getting wilder. I count the seconds between the thunder and lightning so I know when the storm is overhead.

---

handset – Hörer; to shatter – zerbrechen;
to rummage – herumwühlen

There's a thunderstorm at the start of the Rocky Horror Picture Show. The **downpour** is a turning-point for Brad and Janet. They would never have met Dr Frank N. Furter if it hadn't been raining. I wonder whether the ghosts in our cellar will come alive in the storm. The lightning and thunder are almost simultaneous and a shiver runs down my spine. On nights like this **tormented** spirits rise up from their sleep …

Knock knock.

I'm sure I heard someone knocking. There must be someone at the door.

They can't ring the bell because we don't have one (no one does around here) and the ghosts in this village are incredibly polite. It sounds as though they're determined to come in. Who could it be? I cover my ears with my hands. Rocky is asleep on his back, wagging his tail. Thanks, Rocky, you're a great guard dog. Still, even a guard dog couldn't help me fight a ghost. The knocking gets louder until I can hear it through my hands. The front door opens. It opens because we haven't locked the door (they never do around here). I pick up the best **available weapon** – a 30-centimetre wooden ruler – and creep towards my door.

"Annika?"

---

downpour – Platzregen; tormented – gequält;
available – verfügbar; weapon – Waffe

The female ghost knows my name.

"It's me. Mona."

I open my bedroom door. "What are you doing here?"

Mona is **soaked through**. Water drips from her clothes and she looks at me with pleading eyes. "Elsa is having a **calf** and I can't **deliver** it on my own. It's stuck. Mum and Dad are at the parish meeting in Teufelsbrunn and Christian isn't strong enough to help."

I look at Mona and find myself frozen to the spot. She can't seriously be asking me to deliver a calf!

"Please, Annika. The calf will die if you don't help me. So will Elsa."

I pull on my coat. "OK, but we'll have to take Benno with us. I can't leave him here alone. Bennnooo?"

Benno is looking for his Game Boy in the garden. He starts to argue, but then realizes it's serious. We run all the way through the village and to the top of the hill while lightning flashes above us in the sky. It's raining heavily and we can hardly see a thing.

"Doesn't it ever stop raining?" I yell. I can't wait for Mona to open the door so we can **shelter** in the

---

to be soaked through – durchnässt sein;
calf – Kalb; to deliver – *hier:* zur Welt bringen;
to shelter – Schutz suchen

barn. The cow is in trouble, even I know that. It's stamping with its **hind legs** and **bellowing**. We throw our jackets into a corner.

"What do you want me to do?" I don't have a clue. Where the hell do we start?

"We'll have to hurry or she won't make it." Mona keeps calm despite the seriousness of the situation.

"I'll leave you to it," says Benno. "Maybe Christian's got a Game Boy."

"Calves are born with their front legs first," Mona tells me. She starts unrolling a **coil of rope**. "It must be stuck somehow. We'll have to pull it out or give it a **jerk**."

I walk up to Elsa and try to calm her down. I stroke her trembling body and talk quietly to her. "You're having a beautiful little calf. It'll be fine, you'll see. We're here to help you."

"Annika, you've got longer fingernails than me. Stick your hand inside Elsa and tear the **amniotic sac**."

Oh my God. Mona wants me to put my hand inside a cow. I try to keep calm. I'll never be able to tear the amniotic sac. Then again, Mona thinks I can do it, and I don't want to prove her wrong. She

---

barn – Scheune; hind legs – Hinterbeine;
to bellow – brüllen; coil of rope – Seilrolle;
jerk – Ruck; amniotic sac – Fruchtblase

fetches some warm soapy water and I give my arm a wash. I stick my hand carefully inside Elsa, whilst Mona strokes her ears.

"Can you feel it?"

My fingers touch the calf's legs behind a thin layer of skin. I guess that's the amniotic sac then. I use the long fingernail on my index finger to tear slowly through the skin. **Fluid** rushes towards me. *Moo*, says Elsa. I've done it! Mona bends down and ties the rope around the calf's legs. She knots the other end to a wooden post.

"Right, use all your strength. We've got to do this quickly; the calf can't survive without air. One, two, three ..."

We pull as hard as we can.

"We're hurting her!" I cry.

"Keep pulling, Annika! We won't hurt her – I've seen a calf being delivered by a tractor before!"

I try not to think about it and keep pulling instead. Elsa moos. The calf doesn't move, so Mona reaches inside Elsa and **wiggles** its legs.

"We should get Elsa to lie down!" I shout. "Maybe that will help."

We join forces to push Elsa to her knees and make her lie down. We try again.

"We're running out of time!" Tears **stream down**

---

fluid – Flüssigkeit; to wiggle – *hier:* bewegen;
to stream down – herunterströmen

Mona's face. Maybe it's the sight of Mona crying, but I suddenly find new strength. At first nothing happens. The calf won't move. Then there's a jerk, and before we know it, the calf is on the floor. It flies out of Elsa and lies motionless on the straw. Mona cuts the **umbilical cord** and we stare at it.

"Hello, little calf," I whisper **hoarsely**. Suddenly I realize that I'm crying, too. I'm sure the calf is dead. I just know it.

The calf lifts its head.

"It's alive!" Mona throws her arms round me and we cry tears of joy and **snot**. It's alive!

We help the calf to stand up and drink, then we go inside to shower. Warm water streams over my body, and I'm happy for a change. I haven't had a hot shower in weeks, but that's not why I feel so good. No, it's because ... Well, it's because I helped deliver a cow! Just me and Mona – we did it by ourselves! It's a male calf, and Mona names it "Georg". It takes me a while to realize that she's called it the same name as my Georg. Of course, he's not *my* Georg as such – he's just Georg, the guy I work with. I guess it's just **coincidence**.

We drink hot chocolate in the kitchen and Mona lends me some stonewashed jeans and a checked shirt. I don't care about the clothes right

---

umbilical cord – Nabelschnur; hoarse – heiser, rau;
snot – Rotz; coincidence – Zufall

now: there's a new-born calf in the barn and we delivered it! We sit at an old table whose wood has **fed** generations of worms. There's a smell of hot chocolate and shampoo. Bunches of **herbs** are drying by the windows. It's dark enough for Mona to give me a compliment: "Anyone would think you'd done it a hundred times before." She tries to smile.

"Not bad for a city girl, was I?" Oops. Me and my big mouth.

"Sorry," says Mona, disappearing behind her mug.

"Me, too," I say.

"It's not that you're from the city. I mean, well ... The thing is ..." Mona takes a deep breath, and suddenly I know what she's about to say.

"I've got a boyfriend, you know," I cut in.

There's no need to make things **awkward** for her. I can see what all this is about. Mona fancies Georg. I must have been blind not to realize.

Mona stares at me, and I have to go on. "He's called Alex, and he's the best-looking guy in the world. I'm not interested in Georg. I've got Alex." I grin at her. "And **besides**, Alex isn't silent all the time."

Mona smiles back. A great big wide smile. It

---

to feed – *hier:* ernähren; herbs – Kräuter;
awkward – peinlich, unangenehm; besides – außerdem

makes her look pretty. "No one could be better-looking than Georg!" We grin at each other, and the clock strikes half midnight.

"Oh God, I'd better go home. I haven't seen Benno for hours. He must be playing on your brother's Game Boy."

Mona looks **puzzled**. "Christian hasn't got a Game Boy."

I panic. Where the hell is Benno? If Christian hasn't got a Game Boy, Benno must have run away. There's nothing for him to do round here. He could have walked home on his own to dig up Mum's garden. What if he's lost? He could have wandered into the **graveyard** by mistake. Maybe his soul has been stolen by a village ghost who's risen from the dead. In horror stories **tombs** slide open in the middle of storms ... I've lost Benno and I've only just noticed!

"I bet they're up in the **hayloft**," says Mona.

Yeah, right. Benno wouldn't know a hayloft if he saw one. He's not interested in **straw**. Mona takes me by the hand and leads me to a barn. An old light bulb is dangling from the **rafters**. I see a **rickety** old ladder leading to the hayloft. Benno and Christian grin down at us from a big **bale** of straw.

---

puzzled – verblüfft, verdutzt; graveyard – Friedhof; tomb – Grab; hayloft – Heuboden; straw – Stroh; rafter – Dachbalken; rickety – wackelig; bale – Ballen

Update
from the Village Front

Countryside correspondent Annika Weber with all the latest news ...

Once again I'm reporting to you from Höllenhausen, the **flood-prone** location of the Weber family's "jewel". As you can see from the umbrella, the rain hasn't stopped. If Mr Weber had more business sense, he would open the house to the public. He could give guided tours to bus-loads of visitors from Munich. The money could go towards buying a flush for his half-price toilet. Tourists would happily pay for the privilege of seeing a 21st-century family in **medieval** circumstances. The Webers' lifestyle is **genuinely unique**.

A heavy storm swept the valley a few days ago and **wreaked havoc** with the roof. Everyone was out at the time (the two youngest members of the family had gone out to deliver a cow) so no one was home to empty the buckets of water. The next

---

flood-prone – überschwemmungsgefährdet;
medieval – mittelalterlich; genuine – echt, ehrlich;
unique – einzigartig;
to wreak havoc – verheerenden Schaden anrichten

morning the whole house was flooded. Mr Weber decided to solve the problem by removing the roof.

"It's the best way of drying it out," he said.

Unfortunately, the rain showed no sign of stopping and the house got even wetter. The **tarpaulin** roof **proved no match** for nature.

"All this water will be great for my vegetables," remarked Mrs Weber, determined to stay cheerful. She swore never to use **fertilizers** or pesticides on her plants. Her views on gardening contributed to the debacle at last week's parish meeting. The village builders, plumbers and glaziers are now busy until next year.

The meeting got off to an excellent start. Mr and Mrs Weber were keen to adapt to the ways of the community, so Mrs Weber passed round some home-made cookies, signed up for a weekly walk with the village wives, and agreed to take lessons in the art of milking. Mr Weber gave a generous **donation** towards the village **maypole** and raised his glass once too often in honour of new friendships. His **impassioned** speech against the dangers of **artificial** fertilizers and pesticides was met with

---

tarpaulin – Zeltplane;
to prove no match – es nicht aufnehmen können;
fertilizer – Dünger; donation – Spende;
maypole – Maibaum; impassioned – leidenschaftlich;
artificial – künstlich

stony silence. He used the pause in conversation to ask a local builder for an emergency appointment for the roof. The villagers gave the builder death stares and he refused.

Mrs Weber went ahead with her milking lessons. The cow inexplicably kicked her and Mrs Weber had to go to hospital. Mona's mum was in charge of the lessons and offered to give the animal a home on her farm. Mrs Weber turned her down. She had no intention of **being defeated** by a cow, no matter how violent.

The family's relationship with Hermann is equally troubled. Crisis point came when Mr Weber **dozed off** at the dinner table because of chronic lack of sleep. He decided to re-educate the traumatized cockerel. Over the following week he got up at 06.00 and went to the chicken pen to teach Hermann to crow.

"Listen Hermann: six in the morning is the perfect time to crow!"

Privately I have my doubts that six in the morning is the perfect time to do anything but sleep, but Banana Joe turns up with the school bus at seven, so I really can't complain.

Hermann listened attentively to Mr Weber. The family still gets woken at four.

---

to be defeated – besiegt werden;
to doze off – einschlafen

On a more positive note, Hannchen and Helga have demonstrated their usefulness by laying lots of eggs. Mrs Weber, however, feels sorry for the "poor **wee lassies**" and refuses to steal their "babies". Now the Webers are forced to buy their eggs from an organic farmer in a neighbouring village. "At least we don't know the mother," Mrs Weber explained.

In the meantime everyone has **adjusted to** using the outhouse, **despite** the lack of running water. Fortunately, the household is equipped with a rain **barrel** and a **cleaning rota**.

"Everyone has to take their turn. We're going to do this democratically. Do you know what that means, Benno?"

Democracy is a familiar concept to Benno Weber but he couldn't care less. When his oldest playmate, the Game Boy, was banished, he had to find new friends. Christian is a farmer's son and the naughtiest kid in the village. He leaves a trail of destruction behind him. He **hit it off** with Benno right away. "Democracy," announced Mr and Mrs Webers' son, "is when the weak are supported by the strong." He recently smashed

---

wee lassie – kleines Mädchen;
to adjust to – sich anpassen an;
despite – trotz; barrel – Fass, Tonne;
cleaning rota – Putzplan;
to hit it off – sich gut verstehen

the corner-shop window with a home-made catapult.

The lack of running water no longer troubles Annika Weber. Mona's change of heart means she can shower at her house for as long as she likes. To her dog's displeasure, Annika has agreed to take care of Guinea Pig until her brother returns to his senses. Rocky now refuses to leave the house, preferring to **crouch** in front of the cage and wait for Guinea Pig to **venture out**, so he can swallow him **in one go**.

So, dear friends, come and see for yourselves! Isn't Höllenhausen worth a visit? Why not lift your bums from your seats, leave the heat of the city and experience the idyllic charms of the village for yourselves?

You've been listening to Annika Weber, live from the countryside at the heart of the action.

---

to crouch – kauern, lauern;
to venture out – sich hinauswagen;
in one go – auf einmal

Snip, Snap

Janet is feeling confused. She can't believe she's had sex with Rocky, a monster that Dr Frank N. Furter created in his **lab**. Worst of all, she enjoyed it. What about her beloved Brad? She stands in the lab and sings straight from the heart. Her eyes are fixed on me. Johanna is really good at this. She sounds as though she's had singing lessons. I'm **transfixed** by her performance until I notice that Georg is standing behind me. He's so close that I find it difficult not to move. A **tingling** sensation **spreads** from every point of contact, and at first I think he's touching me on purpose whereas actually he doesn't have a choice – he's **hemmed in** by the chairs we've been decorating and the wall. The tingling doesn't stop, though. What if it's a heart attack? There are three good reasons why it can't have anything to do with Georg. Firstly, Alex, not Georg, is the one who makes me tingle. Secondly,

---

lab – Labor; to be transfixed – gebannt sein;
tingling – prickelnd; to spread – sich ausbreiten;
to be hemmed in – eingeklemmt sein

I've arranged to meet Mona so she can charm Georg. And thirdly, it feels like I'm in love and it's obvious that I'm not. Not with Georg, at any rate. I leave that to Mona.

"I've been in love with him for two whole years!" Poor Mona is obsessed.

Mona and I have been friends since the night that we delivered Georg the calf. I told her that I wasn't interested in Georg the guy, and she thanked me for saving Elsa and her baby. Now she lets me shower at her place whenever I like. We usually sit around and chat for a bit beforehand and afterwards. In fact, I even call round when I don't need to use the shower. We drink hot chocolate, listen to some music and hang out together. Mona **mucks out** the cows, feeds the animals, steals eggs from the hens and I sketch her while she works. Her farm is the biggest in the village and everyone has to help. Only Christian gets away with it, but he's a devil child from Höllenhausen. You can't force him to do anything, which reminds me of my brother. The two of them are firm friends.

I've heard every single detail about Mona's **unrequited** love. Apparently, she's tried *everything* to get Georg to notice her. It's no wonder that he hasn't. As far as I can tell, *everything* consists of star-

---

to muck out – ausmisten; unrequited – unerwidert

ing at him admiringly from a distance. She hasn't got any further. She hasn't even spoken to him!

"Er, Mona, I'm not trying to be rude here," I said, "but I don't think you've tried *everything*." Georg might not care about clothes, but even he must have seen the way her shirt is tucked into her jeans. It's not exactly **flattering**.

"Liz Taylor wears checked shirts in her westerns," Mona said **indignantly**.

"**What's your point?**" I asked.

"Pardon?"

"Have you ever been in a western?"

Mona shook her head and frowned.

"There you go then," I told her. "You need to change your look."

"But if Georg likes me, it won't make a difference if I'm wearing a checked shirt!"

I rolled my eyes **in despair**. I don't have much **faith** in inner beauty. Sure, it's a good thing to be a nice person and not be completely **dumb**, but it doesn't hurt to look good, too. "Don't worry. I'll help."

Mona has never had a boyfriend. She was a kid when she fell in love with Georg and he hasn't

---

flattering – schmeichelhaft;
indignant – entrüstet, empört;
What's your point? – Was willst du damit sagen?;
in despair – verzweifelt; faith – Glaube, Vertrauen;
dumb – dumm

paid her any attention since. She's never kissed a boy. That's Mona for you: she's a **single-minded** kind of person. It doesn't **occur to** her to change things and she never tries to be anything but herself. I guess that makes her a good person, but it hasn't got her far with Georg.

"Can you really get Georg to notice me?"

Of course, I can. **No sweat.** I'm from Munich and I'm dating Alex. He's not just any old guy – he's the most popular guy in the school. If anyone knows how to get hold of a man, it's me. OK, so maybe I was feeling a bit **smug** at the time, but I offered to help her change the way she looks.

Mona **scowled**. "I'm happy the way I am."

I picked up a pair of scissors from her desk and held them in the air – snip, snap! "It's nothing to worry about – I'm just going to bring out your **features**." I cut off the long strand of hair that was dangling down her back. It's not cool to have a rat tail.

"That took me five years to grow," she **squealed**.

"Have you ever seen Liz Taylor with a rat tail?"

Mona shook her head. "No way. She's far too feminine."

---

single-minded – zielstrebig, geradlinig;
to occur to sb – jmdm. in den Sinn kommen;
No sweat. – Kein Problem.; smug – eingebildet;
to scowl – ein böses Gesicht machen;
feature – Gesichtszug; to squeal – jammern

Precisely my point.

A bit of hair gel, a few of my clothes, a touch of mascara and hey presto – **tomboy** Mona was a completely new woman. We stood in her bedroom and admired her reflection.

"Now show me a **captivating** smile," I commanded.

Mona gave a **lopsided** grin.

"I said *captivating*!" I gave her a demonstration and soon she was doing it far better than me. We charmed the mirror for a few minutes, then fell about laughing. Mona's eyes were shining, and I was willing to bet that most guys would do anything to date her. Most *normal* guys, that is, but maybe not Georg. Georg is different, so it's difficult to tell. Mona has nothing to lose, though. How's she supposed to get anywhere without giving it a go?

"I'll think of a few tricks to **set things in motion**," I promised.

"Tricks?" Mona was horrified.

"Absolutely! For one thing, you'll have to run into Georg "accidentally" to make sure he notices you."

"But what if he doesn't?"

---

tomboy – Wildfang; captivating – bezaubernd;
lopsided – schief;
to set things in motion – die Dinge ins Rollen bringen

"You'll have to talk to him instead."

I could practically see the question mark on Mona's face. "What would I say?"

"Well, he always needs coins for the drinks machine. You could lend him some change." I put my hand on my heart. "He'll love it if you can give him what he needs. Isn't that what everyone wants from their partners?" I grinned.

"What about Alex then?"

I tried to think. What was special about Alex? His constant activity? To be honest, it wasn't really my thing. His coolness? I shrugged. "You see, Mona, you've got to be cool, or at least, you've got to *seem* cool. You shouldn't smile as soon as he looks at you."

Mona was **taken aback**. "I thought I was supposed to be captivating!"

I sighed. "Not always. It depends! All right: if you need to play it cool, I'll **cough**, OK?"

"OK."

"Bring along a few guys. It's good to seem popular. It makes other guys like you, too."

"That's just depressing."

Typical Mona. Suddenly I realized that everyone fancied Alex, too. But that wasn't why I liked him, of course. It was love at first sight. My heart just

---

to be taken aback – verblüfft sein;
to cough – husten

happened to be **conquered** by the most popular boy in the school.

Johanna sings the final note of Janet's love song. I burst into applause. It's OK to make a noise again, so Georg squeezes out from behind me. Johanna heads over, beaming. "What did you think?"

Mona is **due to** show up at any moment, so I try to keep an eye on the door. "You were amazing! When did you learn to sing like that?"

Johanna blushes. She looks good with her rosy cheeks, blonde hair and cherry-red lips. "Do you mean that? Really?"

I take her hands, hold them firmly and look her in the eye to make sure that she believes me. Johanna could use some **self-esteem**. "If you ask me, you sang better than Janet in the film."

She clasps my hands and glows with pride. A Christmas tree could barely shine any brighter. She looks practically radioactive.

"Annika!"

Mona has appeared at the door. Johanna drops my hands, and I focus my attention on Mona and her burning love for Georg. He won't be able to ignore her for much longer. Mona looks fabulous.

---

to be conquered – erobert werden;
to be due to – sollen, müssen;
self-esteem – Selbstbewusstsein

She flashes me a captivating smile, and Jockel grins over her shoulder. Why on earth did she bring him? I guess he was the best she could do at such short notice. Georg is **stapling** red material to the chairs and doesn't look up. Jockel hands me something. "I made it myself!"

It's a campaign badge with a picture of a slipper. He's crossed it out in red. **Considering** his glasses are totally smeared, he's done a pretty good job.

"Hello, Georg!" Mona must be feeling brave.

"Hello." Georg continues to focus on the chairs.

Mona looks at me doubtfully and her smile starts to fade. That's my cue. I walk over and snatch the stapler away from Georg. "**Let's call it a day.** Why don't we get a hot chocolate?"

Georg looks surprised. He stares at me, then at Mona, and raises his eyebrows. He's obviously noticed her new look.

She beams back and rummages through her pockets. "I can lend you some change."

I groan internally. How would Mona know that Georg needs change? I simulate a coughing **fit** while Mona pretends to look cool. Jockel hands me an **unwrapped** cough sweet. It's covered in **dust**. "You'd better not be getting ill!"

---

to staple – tackern;
considering – wenn man bedenkt, dass;
Let's call it a day. – Lasst uns für heute Schluss machen.;
fit – Anfall; unwrapped – ausgepackt; dust – Staub

Georg sticks his hands in his pockets and seems to brace himself for the events ahead. I push him out of the drama room. "Come on, let's get some proper hot chocolate at the café over the road."

Georg allows himself to be dragged along. Once we're outside, I link arms with Jockel and make sure we lag behind. Georg and Mona walk ahead.

This is the moment that Mona has been **dreading**. "You won't leave me alone with him, will you? What if he goes silent on me?"

"Then *you*'ll have to say something. You never have trouble talking to me."

"But that's different!" Mona looked so unhappy that I helped her with a few ideas – things that I knew Georg was interested in, like horror stories and art. "He loves *Frankenstein*."

Right now it seems Mona's worst fears have been realized. Georg is walking alongside her in silence. Poor Mona! She turns round and looks to me for help. I nod encouragingly, then stop and **tie my laces**. Mona needs to deal with this herself. This is her chance to make an impression. I watch the two of them disappear around the corner and take my time. Jockel waits for me. "What do you think about the campaign badge?" he asks. "If you

---

to dread – fürchten;
to tie one's laces – sich die Schnürsenkel binden

like, we could make a whole load of them and hand them out."

Whilst we're walking, he tells me the details – his ideas for making badges, his plans for a demonstration and his dream of a school in which everyone protests against the tyranny of slippers. I find it hard to concentrate because I can't believe what I'm seeing. A miracle has happened: Mona is deep in conversation with Georg! I'm dying to know what they're talking about. I **speed up**, but Jockel won't stop talking and I can't hear a thing.

"Don't you ever shut up?" I snap at him.

Jockel **stops in his tracks**. "Christ, Annika! You were the one who started the slipper protest. You can't shout at me just because –"

"I know. I'm sorry," I say with a sigh. I search my pockets for the badge and pin it to my sweater. Then I put my arm back through Jockel's and pull him along. Georg and Mona haven't bothered to wait. I don't think they'd notice if a bottomless crater opened up in the road and **sucked** us into **infinity** to join the army of ghosts. **Neither** would Jockel. He'd still be talking about badges whilst he **plummeted** through the air.

We get to the café and order four mugs of hot

---

to speed up – schneller werden;
to stop in one's tracks – stehen bleiben;
to suck – ziehen, saugen; infinity – Unendlichkeit;
neither – auch nicht; to plummet – abstürzen

chocolate. Whilst the guys pick some cake from the **counter**, I take the chance to **interrogate** Mona. I'm dying of curiosity. "What were you talking about?"

Mona beams. Her cheeks are red with excitement. "We didn't say anything at first. My mind went blank. It was too awful for words. Then we walked past a poster of a cow and I told him about Georg the calf. He was dead impressed that we delivered it on our own. The same thing happened to him once. He thinks the moment of birth is really amazing."

Jesus, you can tell these guys grew up on farms! "Did you tell him its name?" I ask, grinning.

"No, I don't think she **mentioned** it. What's it called?"

I **swivel round** and come face to face with Georg and Jockel. My cheeks go redder than Mona's. I need to say something, but what?

Mona doesn't **hesitate**: "We called it Frankenstein!"

"Cool!" Georg plumps down next to her.

"It's my favourite book," she explains.

My jaw drops. For a farmer's daughter who's never had a boyfriend she's pretty damn good. So

---

counter – Theke; to interrogate – ausfragen;
to mention – erwähnen;
to swivel round – sich herumdrehen;
to hesitate – zögern

much for **rural** naivety! Mona pulls a well-worn novel from her bag. "I take it everywhere. You should read it some time."

It works. Georg and Mona are back in conversation again. Mona seems to know every last detail about the book. She must have learned it off by heart. Village kids aren't as innocent as you think.

Jockel interrupts my thoughts. "Maybe we can start a petition at the counter. What do you **reckon**?" I let him get on with it. He gives me his sugar **sachet** because I can't find mine and disappears to the counter. I keep **stirring** my hot chocolate until every last **granule** of sugar has dissolved.

There's a poem on my wall. I tacked it midway between the gherkin shelf and my mattress, so it's exactly at eye-level when I'm lying down.

If I were a stone,
I'd ***crumble*** *before you.*
If I were a giant,
I'd kneel at your feet.
If I were the Rhine,
I'd wrap myself around you
And never let go.

---

rural – ländlich; to reckon – glauben, denken;
sachet – Tütchen; to stir – umrühren;
granule – Körnchen; to crumble – zerfallen

It arrived three days ago in the post. The envelope was addressed to me – an anonymous love poem in a plain white envelope. There was something **understated** about it that reminded me of Georg.

I rip the poem off the wall and put it in a drawer. Georg isn't understated or unapproachable. Georg fancies Mona. He wouldn't write a love poem for me. Besides, I wouldn't want a poem from Georg. What the hell was I thinking? I must be mad.

It's dinnertime and Mum and Dad are arguing in the kitchen. Benno has disappeared. He's hardly ever at home. He spends most of his time with Christian, causing trouble. These days he loves climbing trees and never mentions his Game Boy.

"Isn't that what we wanted?" asks Mum.

Dad shakes his head. "I don't see why he has to go to the opposite extreme. Can't he do anything **in moderation**? I guess he takes after you."

"I'm not extreme!" shouts Mum. Her voice is extremely loud and extremely **screechy**.

I can barely hear myself think, so I offer to look for Benno. Rocky comes, too, and the air does us good. What could be better than fresh country air that smells of nothing except the occasional cow?

Was it wrong of me to think that someone who

---

understated – schlicht; in moderation – in Maßen; screechy – kreischend

isn't my boyfriend might write me a poem? Alex hasn't called for ages. Maybe he's guessed about the poem and can sense I was secretly pleased. I **tell** myself **off** for being ridiculous. His parents have probably banned him from calling because of the bill.

I wander over to my bench and look out from the top of the hill. It's not Monday, so Alex and Suse won't be on the viewing platform. Maybe Alex will guess what I'm thinking anyway. Maybe he can sense that I love him, that we're meant for each other and that nothing can …

Bang! A rubber arrow hits the back of my head and sticks to my hair. Rocky is barking like mad. Normally I'd wonder whether a village ghost had shot me, but Benno and Christian are already storming towards me. They're **bare-chested** and wearing cut-off jeans (from what I can tell, they cut them off themselves) and they're covered from head to toe in mud. I think it's supposed to be **camouflage**.

Apparently, they want to spend the night out here and defend the village against enemy attacks. It's a nice idea, but Big Sister has to **intervene**. I drag the muddy **warrior** back home.

---

to tell oneself off – sich selbst ausschimpfen;
bare-chested – mit nacktem Oberkörper;
camouflage – Tarnung; to intervene – eingreifen;
warrior – Krieger

There's no hot water, so Benno takes a bath in the rain barrel.

Our cow is **grazing** nearby. I stare at her. There's a great big heart on her side. Someone has written my name on our cow. Who could it be? I guess I should **feel flattered**. Not everyone receives love letters written on a cow. I'm probably the only one, in fact. But all these anonymous messages are making me nervous. I can't believe anyone could love me enough to risk Mum's rage by writing all over her cow.

"Look at the state of that animal!" Mum rushes into the yard. "Annika, you're to clean that mess up immediately, do you hear?"

Now that's just great. Thanks a billion, my secret admirer!

---

to graze – grasen;
to feel flattered – sich geschmeichelt fühlen

No Contest

Right, that **settles** it. I've decided to go to Munich. I haven't told Alex yet. I'll just show up on his doorstep and remind him why I'm such a great girlfriend. Annika Weber is the world's best kisser, no contest.

"Sorry, Annika, I don't have time to talk!" Alex could **barely** get rid of me fast enough. I'd phoned him, of course. We hadn't talked for ages, and then he couldn't wait to finish the call. So it's settled: I'm going to Munich. I can't wait to see his face.

Mona and Georg are coming, too. It's the next stage in my matchmaking plan. I'll visit Alex, and the two of them can wander around the city. If romance doesn't **blossom** in a place like Munich, it never will. Georg didn't need much **persuading**.

"Why don't we go to Munich and watch the

---

contest – Wettkampf; to settle – *hier:* entscheiden;
barely – kaum; to blossom – sich entfalten;
to persuade – überzeugen

Rocky Horror Picture Show at the movies. **We could do with** the inspiration." I made it sound like a suggestion but my mind was made up.

Georg nodded in agreement. Thanks to him the school even paid for our trip. His logic was **impeccable**. "It's for research **purposes**," he told Mr Schmidt-Bürste. "We're trying to make our production as authentic as possible. It's an audience-participation show. We want our audience to identify with the characters like they do when they watch the film. We need to see how it works. I'm sure you understand."

Schmidt-Bürste is our Latin teacher, but he's also school **treasurer**. He saw his opportunity. "Maybe Annika would like to reconsider her slipper protest ..."

Unbelievable! I was being **blackmailed** by a teacher!

Georg saved the day. "But sir, our research trip has nothing to do with Annika's shoes. I know you'd never try to blackmail us."

Mr S-B unlocked the **minuscule** school safe with a tiny key. He counted out some notes with a **tight-lipped** smile. He wouldn't pay for Mona, of

---

We could do with sth. – Wir könnten etwas brauchen.;
impeccable – *hier:* bestechend;
purpose – Zweck;
treasurer – Kassenwart; to blackmail – erpressen;
minuscule – winzig; tight-lipped – schmallippig

course, but she didn't mind. Anything to spend more time with Georg!

Johanna wanted to come, too. "I'm playing Janet. I should see the movie, too!"

Jockel was practically packed and ready to go. "You're not going without me, Annika!"

There wasn't room for Jockel in the plan. Luckily, I managed to talk him into staying behind for the slipper resistance. Johanna had a rehearsal so she couldn't come anyway. She took my hand. "You'll have to tell me about it." I made a **solemn** promise and it seemed to do the trick.

We've planned our visit for Monday. Lessons have been cancelled because the school needs new carpets. God knows what's wrong with the old ones – they can't exactly be dirty because everyone wears slippers. I'm not complaining, though. Monday suits me fine. Alex and Suse will be at the television tower, so I'll turn up and surprise them. I can't believe I'm on my way to Munich.

Mona and I took ages getting ready but Georg is wearing paint-stained jeans. I guess he doesn't care about impressing anyone with his outfit. That's just the way he is. And anyway, he can get away with it: he's got the most amazing butt in the world. Right now his bum is making its way down the train as he walks ahead of us with three cups

---

solemn – feierlich

of **cocoa**. Mona and I stare unashamedly. I try to remind myself that a great butt isn't everything. Alex doesn't really have one, but nobody's perfect. And it's only a bottom, for crying out loud.

Munich station is full of people. I **immerse** myself **in** the atmosphere, the noise, the continual announcements, the electronic beeps of the luggage trucks, the hordes of travellers from all over the world, the smells, the shouting – it's just heavenly. The village station has only two platforms, and you're allowed to walk over the rails. Farmers and locals are the only ones who ever get on and off there. Outsiders never use the station, so it doesn't matter if it closes when it snows. In any case, the villagers hardly ever want to leave.

Munich is my home, but it's the big wide world for Mona and Georg. I describe the way to the city centre, "You'll be able to visit the Cathedral of our Lady, St Peter's Church or the Karl Valentin Museum. There's loads to see."

Mona smiles and links arms with Georg. "Don't worry about us! We'll see you at five at the cinema." She drags him away.

Mona doesn't know it yet, but she's a natural. She knows exactly how to act around men. She just puts her arm through Georg's and expects him to protect her. I watch them disappear. Two village

---

cocoa – Kakao; to immerse oneself in – eintauchen in

kids in the city, swallowed by the crowd. In the city they're just nameless people like everyone else.

It's quarter to three. I haven't got much time. I don't want Alex and Suse to leave before I get there.

I run up to the television tower, panting for breath. It looks unbelievably tall when you see it from below. It's five to three already. Alex and Suse will be gazing out from the viewing platform and thinking of me. I expect they're feeling sorry for me because I live in the middle of nowhere where there's nothing to do. They'd be amazed if they knew.

I get into the elevator. It's just me and the conductor. A woman's voice comes through the loudspeakers, telling us how tall the tower is. Blah blah blah. I'm too excited to listen. In fact, I'm too excited to think. Before I know it, my eyes have clouded over and the conductor turns into Riff Raff from the Rocky Horror Picture Show. The noise of his evil laughter echoes through the elevator. He's taking me straight to hell where the village ghosts will grab at my legs with their **spindly** fingers.

"Viewing platform! Please **disembark**!"

My knees wobble as I leave the lift. In a few seconds I'll see Alex. I've been longing for this mo-

---

spindly – spindeldürr; to disembark – aussteigen

ment ever since we moved. I'm going to tap him on the shoulder and pretend to be annoyed. "Excuse me, young man, but you're not the only one round here who'd like to see the view!"

Alex will **whip round** and start to answer back, but then his frown will **vanish** and he'll smile. He'll touch my face to make sure that I'm real. Then we'll kiss.

He's not here. I've walked round the platform three times now, and the only other person is a toothless old man. "Woads, wivers and fields. Look at that view ..." he **lisped**.

Roads, rivers and fields – precisely. My best friend and my boyfriend promised to be here every Monday to look at the view and think of me. It's ten minutes past three already. Surely they can't have gazed into the distance, thought of me and left already? No, they're not here now and they weren't here beforehand. Something must have happened. I talked to Suse recently, and she told me how they always come here and imagine that I'm with them, too.

On my way to Alex's house I worry about what could have gone wrong. Maybe Alex has been **grounded** by his parents. Or maybe he's had an ac-

---

to whip round – herumwirbeln;
to vanish – verschwinden; to lisp – lispeln;
to be grounded – Hausarrest haben

cident. He could be in hospital, fighting for his life. Tears pour down my cheeks. I should have seen it coming. Alex always tries to do a million things at once. He probably ran out into the road and – bam! – he was hit by a car.

His mum could have left them, I guess. Maybe Alex is at home comforting his dad. I knock at the door and Alex's mum opens. She hasn't gone back to India after all. She seems really pleased to see me. "Annika! What a lovely surprise! They won't believe their eyes …"

Their eyes?

I go straight upstairs. Alex and Suse pull away from each other as soon as I open the door. Too late. I've seen enough already. My best friend and my boyfriend were rolling around on the bed in a passionate **embrace**. They were kissing – **French kissing**. I stand there, frozen to the spot. Suse straightens her T-shirt and Alex **scrambles up** but overbalances, landing on his non-existent butt. "Annika! What –"

Suse can't think of what to say. I hardly ever stop talking, but in her place I'd probably be speechless, too. I half expect her to come out with something positive. *Look on the bright side – at least we weren't naked or anything …*

---

embrace – Umarmung; French kissing – Zungenkuss;
to scramble up – sich hochrappeln

"Uh, what are you doing here?" Alex finally manages to sit up.

Suddenly I'm not frozen any more. My whole body **teems with life**. This is my worst nightmare and it hurts.

"If only you'd been hit by a car!" I scream at Alex. I'd rather see him in hospital than catch him kissing Suse. How could she do this to me? I'm her best friend.

They look at me, and no one says a word. There's nothing to say. They don't have an explanation: things are *exactly* as they seem.

"Go ahead and stare then. You won't be seeing me again!" I run out of the room, slam the door behind me and collide with Alex's mum. Biscuits fly everywhere. I don't have time to say sorry. Why should I? Anyone who gives birth to a son like that doesn't deserve an apology.

I run out of the house and stop in a neighbour's doorway. I can't run any further. My legs have turned to jelly, my heart is aching and all I can see is darkness. I sit on the ground and **scrunch** myself into a ball. I'm not here. This can't be happening to me. It just can't. I trusted them and they **betrayed** me. They were my future, my home. I built my dreams on them, and they can't even be

---

to teem with life – sich mit Leben füllen;
to scrunch – zusammenrollen; to betray – verraten

bothered to look for me. There's no point hiding in a doorway – they're not interested in where I am. The street is full of passers-by. I stare at the procession of legs and can't bring myself to move. After a while I see Suse's legs, too. Her face is red from crying, but I don't feel sorry for her. She and Alex can do what they like. I'd be better off without their friendship. I **give** myself **a pep talk** and at last I'm ready to stand up and leave.

Right now I couldn't care less about the Rocky Horror Picture Show. I've got my own living nightmare and crying in a doorway isn't going to help. I thought I could trust my friends but I was wrong. I'll just have to get on with life. As I walk through the city, I wonder if the tramps in the doorways are unhappy people who've been **abandoned** by their loved ones. I feel sure of it. I drop my last bit of change into a beggar's hat. No more hot chocolates for Georg.

Munich is noisy and grey. It's weird but I don't feel like crying. The station is warm and stuffy and it stinks in the underground. I walk to the cinema instead. Hopefully Mona and Georg will have found their way there. My **rose-tinted** glasses are gone. I've been an idiot. Firstly, I should never have left two village kids alone in the city. How the

---

to give oneself a pep talk – sich aufbauen;
to abandon – im Stich lassen; rose-tinted – *hier:* rosarot

hell were they supposed to make it to the cinema? And secondly, why did I ever think that Georg would fall for Mona just because they're in Munich? What a pathetic idea.

I'm half an hour late by the time I get to the cinema. The woman at the ticket desk refuses to let me in.

"Just let me take a look inside then. I'm sure my friends won't be there. I'll come straight back out, I promise."

I come straight back out, as promised.

Mona and Georg are in the front row – kissing.

Update
from the Village Front

Countryside correspondent Annika Weber with all the latest news ...

Waterproof overalls are mostly seen on fishermen, but these days everyone in Höllenhausen is wearing them.

This is Annika Weber reporting from the rural front.

Well, the rain is just about the only thing the **residents** of Höllenhausen can rely on. Everything else continues to **spiral out of control**. But maybe that's the point about chaos: it just gets worse and worse.

Mr Weber has been struggling to **cope with** the never-ending rain. Experts are talking of a "millennial downpour". Mr Weber can take comfort in the fact that he'll be dead before it rains like this again. All the same, the timing is terrible: the **deluge** arrived while the house had no roof. Urgent action was required.

---

waterproof – wasserdicht; resident – Einwohner;
to spiral out of control – immer mehr außer Kontrolle geraten;
to cope with – es aufnehmen mit; deluge – Flut

Mr Weber **racked his brains** and did some sums. His wife added, subtracted and started again. With the help of a new calculator, she finally worked out how many tiles would be needed. They agreed on a plan: Mr Weber would build the frame before the tiles were delivered. The tiles arrived unexpectedly early after only two days. There were far too many of them and Mr Weber hadn't built the frame. He didn't know how. Now the Webers' "jewel" is stacked from top to bottom with tiles. It was cheaper to buy them by the dozen, and most were slightly damaged. You get what you pay for, of course.

The ground floor is relatively dry, although moving around is more of a problem. The local plumber was hired to fix a **blockage** in the hall. He took up the **floorboards** and laid a new pipe. Then Mr Weber saw the estimated bill and refused to pay a penny. The plumber left without finishing the job, so the Webers have running water but no floor.

"I expect your father will fix it," said Mrs Weber. She seemed more doubtful than before.

"Why not use tiles instead of floorboards?" suggested Annika Weber. "I think we've got some **spares**." No one shared her sense of humour.

---

to rack one's brains – sich den Kopf zerbrechen; blockage – Verstopfung; floorboard – Diele; spares – *hier:* Übrige

Still, running water is a definite improvement. It's a little muddy-looking and doesn't get you clean, but at least the toilet flushes properly. And who cares if the toilet flush is brown?

"The colour is ideal," **exclaimed** Annika Weber. She flushed the toilet for the tenth time because she couldn't quite believe it.

"I can't wait to get rid of the outhouse," said Mr Weber.

Mrs Weber disagreed. "You can't knock down the poor outhouse. Just think how many people have used it in their hour of need!"

The rest of the family felt Mrs Weber was taking her social conscience too far. Their protests were **in vain**. If Mrs Weber **had her way**, the **parish council** would honour the outhouse with a historical **plaque**. The oldest toilet in the village deserved to be protected.

"I guess she's feeling guilty about the **slugs**," said Mr Weber, trying to rationalize his wife's behaviour. Her fertilizer- and pesticide-free vegetables had been eaten by slugs. They'd **ransacked** the garden and left nothing but **stalks**.

Mrs Weber **retaliated** with one of the most bru-

---

to exclaim – ausrufen; in vain – umsonst;
to have one's way – seinen Willen durchsetzen;
parish council – Gemeinderat; plaque – Schild;
slug – Schnecke; to ransack – herfallen über;
stalk – Stängel; to retaliate – sich rächen

tal anti-slug campaigns in the history of the world. She drowned them in beer, cut them in half with scissors and took any measures necessary to ensure they didn't reproduce. Her revenge was brutal.

"Slugs are living creatures, too," Annika Weber reminded her.

She timed her comment badly. Mrs Weber turned her anger away from the slugs and focused on her daughter. Mr Weber was the next to feel her fury. Mrs Weber held him responsible for moving to this "**godforsaken** place". Hadn't they been happy in the city? Besides, if he'd joined the stupid rifle club they'd be able to find a builder and get a discount from the plumber.

Mr Weber swallowed his anger. He reached across the table and held his wife's hand. "You're tired, darling. I'll do the milking tomorrow while you have a lie-in."

Despite the other problems, the milking is going to plan. Unfortunately, it takes place at four in the morning, straight after Hermann's pre-dawn chorus. By the time Mr Weber and the children have rolled over, muttered "Good morning Hermann" and gone back to sleep, Mrs Weber is already in the cowshed. She finishes milking, then checks up on Hannchen and Helga and looks for **hatched** eggs. Her search goes unrewarded. Mrs Weber suspects

---

godforsaken – gottverlassen; hatched – ausgebrütet

Hermann of being impotent and takes her frustration out on him. She leaves the chicken pen and strides through the garden to **mutilate** some slugs.

Given the circumstances, Mrs Weber was grateful for her husband's offer of help. Little did she know that her lie-in would be interrupted. Her husband was unable to extract a single drop of milk, and the cow was mooing angrily.

"I knew this would happen," Mrs Weber said triumphantly. "I didn't take lessons for nothing!" Over the next three days she gave her husband an intensive course in milking.

Guinea Pig has become depressed with life in the darkened larder under the **hostile** gaze of the dog. It refuses to come out of its cage and spends its time dreaming of New Guinea and a brighter future.

Lastly, Benno Weber has learned to climb trees. His parents' excitement was short-lived. How were they to know that he was building a tree house with Christian? Benno and Christian intend to live in the woods for as long as they can.

You've been listening to Annika Weber, live from the countryside at the heart of the action.

---

to mutilate – verstümmeln; hostile – feindselig

A and X FOR EVER

I've only just woken up and I'm seeing red already. It's got nothing to do with the frog that's staring me calmly in the face and giving the occasional **croak**. Benno must have put it there. He really fancies himself as a practical joker. The reason why I'm seeing red isn't even because my parents are yelling at each other outside my door. They're arguing about **whose turn it is** to do the milking …

Mum: "Look at the date! It's an ***odd* number**. You always do odd numbers!"

Dad: "That's not fair, darling. Yesterday was an odd number, too."

Mum: "Don't be **petty**. I'm sure I'll do just as much as you **in the long run**."

Dad: "But that's just it! Yesterday was the 31st and today is the 1st. That's two odd days in a row. You never get two even days. It doesn't work like that!"

---

croak – Quaken; whose turn it is – wer an der Reihe ist;
odd number – ungerade Zahl;
petty – kleinlich, engstirnig;
in the long run – auf lange Sicht

Mum: "We had an agreement, remember?"

Dad: "You're unbelievable. I hate to think what a fuss you'd make if you had to do the odds."

Mum: "I don't, though."

Dad: "All I'm suggesting is that we take it in turns. I'll do the odds for the **even** months, and in odd months you'll do the evens. No, wait a minute, I mean the odds."

Mum: "What if it's a **leap year** ..."

No, the reason why I'm seeing red is because someone has covered my window in red paint. The whole window is red except for a bit in the middle that's shaped like a heart. I gaze through it and see the raindrops.

At first I think it must be Alex. God knows why. Probably because the heart looks like the one he drew on my sneakers. I bet I was dreaming about him last night. Before I can stop myself, I start to visualize a film. The hero is a guy called Alex. In a moment of madness he cheats on the woman of his dreams. He keeps calling her to apologize but she pretends she's not there. After a while he can't stand it any longer. He runs outside and tries to **hitch a lift**. Cars speed past him in the dark but eventually someone gives him a ride. At last he's on his way east to the village that he looked at

---

even – gerade; leap year – Schaltjahr;
to hitch a lift – per Anhalter fahren

longingly from the television tower. The driver drops him off in the middle of nowhere. He stumbles through the sleeping village amid the pouring rain. Suddenly he hears a cock crow. The sky is still dark. "That must be Hermann!" he whispers, following the ***cock-a-doodle-doo*** to a decrepit old house. He's found it at last! He looks through a **rickety** window. The moon shines through the tiny pane of glass and lights up the face of his beloved. A cloud passes overhead and darkness returns. He starts to knock on the window, then hesitates. Should he wake his beautiful girlfriend? What will she say to the man who broke her heart? Maybe he should give her a sign of his love. That way she'll know he's sorry …

I shoot out of bed as though a gang of village ghosts has crept under the **duvet**. The frog leaps onto the gherkin shelf as I run to the window, open it and gaze out into the rain. Nothing. No sign of our hero. Alex isn't there. I see two chickens, a cockerel and some sorry-looking vegetables. The cool country air clears my head, and I know straight away that it couldn't have been Alex. He didn't write the poem and he didn't paint the cow.

Anyway, Alex could be dead for all I care. The same goes for Suse. I got a letter from her yester-

---

cock-a-doodle-doo – Kikeriki; rickety – *hier:* vergammelt; duvet – Bettdecke

day. It came in a great big envelope – page after page of explanations I imagine. I expect she wanted to tell me how Robbie Williams wasn't good enough for her and she had to have Alex. *My* Alex. I almost opened it, but I was scared I might forgive her. I don't want to forgive anyone. I want Suse and Alex out of my life.

I **tore up** the letter and stuffed it in one of my sneakers – the one with Suse's 'A' for anarchy. I grabbed the other one, balanced them both on a **plank** and **launched** them down the river. I imagined how the plank would sail out of the village and **drift** on the **current**, carrying my sneakers past meadows, fields and villages until it reached the Isar. **Propelled** by my **will-power**, it would fight its way upstream to Munich, where it would sail into the English Garden and take Alex and Suse by surprise. The sight of my shoes would stop them roller blading or kissing or whatever. The shame would be too much for them and they would never see each other again.

We eat breakfast and I drag myself out of the house. Another surprise is **in store for** me. Outside the front door is an enormous puddle and someone has scattered red roses in the water. They're

---

to tear up – zerreißen; plank – Brett;
to launch – *hier:* vom Stapel lassen; to drift – treiben;
current – Strömung; to propel – antreiben;
will-power – Willenskraft; to be in store for – warten auf

drifting apart but you can tell they were in the shape of a heart.

"How romantic!" sighs Benno. He stomps straight through the middle of the puddle. "Do you mean to say that someone might want you as their girlfriend?"

"**Moron**!" I kick the puddle and spray him with water. That will teach him to put frogs in my bed and make stupid comments.

Benno just smiles and starts to run. When did he learn to move that fast?

I **quicken my pace** and start to think. Would anyone want me as their girlfriend? Who? I'm not sure I really want to know. I'm through with love. I never want anything to do with it again.

It's different for Mona. She waves at me from the bus stop. Her love story has only just begun. It started three days ago at the Rocky Horror Picture Show. She told me about it that evening while we waited for the bus from the station. Georg had already left on his moped. Mona's cheeks were flushed.

"Annika hasn't seen Alex for ages," she'd told Georg when I didn't turn up at the cinema. "She's probably forgotten the time."

"I guess so." The film was about to start so they

---

moron – Trottel, Blödmann;
to quicken one's pace – schneller gehen

went in without me and couldn't believe how cool the cinema was inside. It was decorated to look like a Rocky-Horror style castle, and the seats were full of people who'd seen the film a hundred times before. It's fun but kind of spooky to sit there with people who are all dressed up like phantoms. The real action starts when the film gets going. The audience throws rice during the part when Brad and Janet get married, and everyone gets out their water pistols when the couple start running through the rain. Mona and Georg were soaked and nearly died of laughter. Because everything was so amazing, Mona did something unusually brave. She put her hand on the armrest and brushed against Georg. Her heart was pounding and she thought Georg would move, but he didn't. They held hands and then they kissed.

Now Mona's a new person. I can tell by the way that she's waving that she's **basking in** the joys of love and floating around in seventh heaven. I wave back in a broken-hearted sort of way.

"I heard about the roses. How sweet!" she says.

Benno must have told everyone already. Now he's climbing on the roof of the **bus shelter** with Christian.

"Do you know who it was?"

"The same person who decorated our cow and

---

to bask in – schwelgen in; bus shelter – Bushäuschen

painted a heart on my window," I say in a bored voice.

"I'd be dying of curiosity if I were you. No one's ever done a thing like that for me."

Mona looks at me expectantly. I think she's feeling guilty because things have worked out for her. Everything would be easier if I fell in love again. Well, sorry, Mona, but it's not that simple. Luckily, Joe turns up with the bus, so I let the matter drop.

"Morning, Joe," says Mona.

"Morning, Mona," he says brightly.

"Good morning," I say.

Joe growls. He looks as though a gang of kids have marked his seats with chocolate-covered fingers.

"What's his problem?" Mona whispers.

I shrug, but it doesn't take long to **figure out**. Someone has **sewn** a red heart to the back of the seat in front of me and embroidered *A and X FOR EVER* in white **thread**.

Seconds later Joe appears in the aisle beside me. "Who's responsible for this?" he demands, bending over to take a closer look.

"How should I know?" I say. Surely these people have better things to think about? I'm bored of hearing the same old question.

---

to figure out – verstehen, begreifen;
to sew – nähen; thread – Faden

"Don't mess with me, young lady," snaps Joe. "Out with it! Tell me who it was."

"Seriously, Joe, I don't know," I groan.

"I do!" **pipes up** Benno. He waits until he has everyone's attention. The **suspense** is **unbearable**. "It was X!"

Joe digs his nicotine fingers into the seat. "I'm warning you!"

"But it says so right here!" protests Benno with a **sly** wink. "X ... It must be an **initial**. X for Xavier or for ... What other names begin with X?"

Joe looks as though he might explode. I can't help laughing and Christian joins in. Mona tries to keep a straight face but bursts out laughing, too. Joe glares at Benno, then me, then Christian, then back at Benno. He finally **gives in** and focuses on me: "Tell Mr X from me that he won't be laughing once I get hold of him!" Growling angrily he marches away, sits down behind the wheel and looks at me **threateningly** in the **rear view mirror**. I hear the **gears crunch** as we move away.

On the way to school I pretend to be revising for our Latin test. In reality I'm wondering who would risk Joe's **wrath** by sewing a heart on one of his

---

to pipe up – *hier:* sich einmischen; suspense – Spannung; unbearable – unerträglich; sly – verschmitzt; initial – Anfangsbuchstabe; to give in – nachgeben; threatening – drohend; rear view mirror – Rückspiegel; gear – Gang; to crunch – krachen; wrath – Zorn

seats. They'd have to be seriously in love with me. Who would be brave or crazy enough to do a thing like that? All of a sudden, I find myself thinking of Georg. I can't get him out of my head. What if it was him?

I hear Mona humming one of Janet's soppy love songs and I feel a **stab** of pain – it's an acute case of **guilty conscience**. Georg is Mona's boyfriend. *Culpa* means guilt. *Ratio* means reason. I fill my head with Latin vocabulary to drown out the thought of Georg. Anyhow, so much for *ratio*. Georg is dating Mona. He wouldn't send messages to me!

Mona hums and beams. She's a vision of love. I unpick the **stitches** and rip the heart off the seat. What does it matter who put it there? Love doesn't interest me at the moment. I get back to my vocabulary. Joe **pulls up** in front of the school and we **pile out** into the fresh country air.

"Hey, what's going on over there?" We walk towards the entrance and Mona points to a crowd of pupils **gathered** outside the school. They're laughing, chatting excitedly and staring at the wall.

"Maybe Jockel called a meeting for the slipper resistance," I suggest. We **head over** to take a clos-

---

stab – Stich; guilty conscience – schlechtes Gewissen;
stitch – Stich (einer Naht); to pull up – stoppen;
to pile out – hinausdrängen; to gather – sich versammeln;
to head over – hinübergehen

er look. We push our way through the crowd and at last we see the wall. My heart nearly stops. The clean, white, **untarnished** school wall isn't clean, white and untarnished. It looks like a proper school wall, a wall in an inner city school. I stare at the enormous red letters: *LET LOVE BE OUR ENERGY*. The message ends with a heart and *A and X*. It's the title of a Robbie William's song. Imagine if Suse could see it!

"Come on, Annika," says Mona, "you must know who it is."

"Believe me, I don't," I say moodily. My heart almost stops again. Georg is standing next to the wall with an **aerosol can** in his hand.

Mona must have seen him, too. Her smile vanishes and gives way to a nervous twitch. Surely it can't have been ...?

Georg spots us, too. He walks towards us. It takes five or six paces but it seems like an eternity. The air has turned to thick, **gooey** syrup. I try to read his expression, and I can tell that Mona is doing likewise. We're like two adversaries in court, waiting for the judge to deliver a **verdict**. Georg's face gives nothing away.

"It's one of ours," he says, waving the aerosol.

---

untarnished – unbefleckt;
aerosol can – Sprühdose; gooey – klebrig;
verdict – Urteil

"Someone stole it from the drama room. Bloody moron!"

Mona has won. Her grin returns. "You'll never guess who that moron **has got the hots for**!"

Georg turns to the wall, thinks for a moment, then looks at me. "Maybe he's not such a moron after all." He smiles a sad little smile.

"If you ask me," says Mona, "he's obviously got **impeccable** taste." She **prods** me in the ribs, then turns to kiss Georg.

So much for his sad little smile! I must have been kidding myself. I watch them kiss. It feels worse than seeing Alex and Suse together. Now I'm really alarmed at myself.

"Uh, I'll see you guys later," I **stutter**. "I'd better finish revising for that Latin test." I run off in the direction of our classroom. You're crazy, I keep telling myself. I can't believe what I'm feeling. Georg is just a village kid, and besides, he's Mona's boyfriend. How can I be so stupid?

I flop down at my desk, exhausted by all the thinking, feeling and emotional **wrangling** I've been doing. I put my head in my hands and come face to face with another message. Suddenly I'm wide awake again.

---

to have got the hots for – stehen auf;
impeccable – tadellos; to prod – stoßen;
to stutter – stottern; wrangling – Gerangel, Hin und Her

Someone has crossed through the word *ALEX* and drawn a heart. A heart and some initials inside it … I can't believe my eyes. *J 4 A …*

J?

"Have you heard who's joined the slipper resistance?" Jockel plonks his bag down on to his desk and sits down next to me.

Of course! *J for Jockel.* I cover the heart **casually** with my hand. I don't want him to know that I've seen it.

"Have a guess!" Jockel seems pleased with himself.

I shrug. "Who?"

"Johanna!" he announces, beaming all over his face.

I glance at Johanna. She points to her feet and smiles. She's wearing **high-heeled** boots instead of slippers. That makes four of us – me, Jockel, Mona and Johanna.

"Congratulations," I say to Jockel. "How did you do it?"

"Incredible powers of **persuasion**," he **boasts**, searching through his bag for his books.

Wow. I've got to **hand it to** him. First he tells me that he loves me, then he acts completely cool.

---

casually – beiläufig; high-heeled – hochhackig; persuasion – Überzeugungskraft; to boast – angeben; to hand it to sb – jmdm. etwas zugestehen

We're supposed to be learning algebra but my thoughts are elsewhere. I keep glancing at my not-so-secret admirer. It was a **neat** way of telling me. First the love poem (I would never have thought that Jockel wrote poetry!), then the cow and the window. And it was all completely anonymous, too. Next up were the puddle, the bus and the wall. The last two hearts were signed *X* – still no signature, but at least it got me thinking. *X and A*. Two people who belong together. I'd been curious **in spite of myself**. And now the grand finale – *J 4 A*.

A for Annika, J for Jockel.

"Why don't I have a word with Emil? Maybe he'll join us," he whispers.

I nod and stare ahead. I don't want him to know I was staring at him.

It *must* have been Jockel. I mean, who else could *J* stand for? I guess it was obvious. He's been nice to me from day one. He's my right-hand man in the slipper resistance. He was so disappointed when he couldn't come to Munich.

"Annika, tell us what happens when you add a **property** to both sides of an **equation**!"

Suddenly I'm back in the world of mathematics.

---

neat – *hier:* gelungen;
in spite of myself – gegen meinen Willen;
property – *hier:* beliebige Zahl;
equation – Gleichung

Mr Ziegler has caught me unprepared. I don't know anything about equations. Can't he see that I'm busy? Algebra is the last thing on my mind.

"Well, if you uh … " I stutter.

"Refusing to wear slippers is one thing but not paying attention is another. This won't look good on your **report**!"

Jockel hands me a note. Mr Ziegler is too busy scowling at me to notice. Thanks to Jockel I know the answer.

"I mean, if a = b, then a + c = b + c." I smile brightly at Ziegler. "Just because I don't wear slippers doesn't mean I'm stupid."

"You ought to watch what you say, young lady. One of these days you could find yourself in trouble." Ziegler turns back to the white board.

"Thanks," I whisper to Jockel.

Maths isn't the only thing he's good at. He's a nice person and he's sweet, kind and funny. Too bad about his smeared glasses and his non-existent hairstyle.

"Can I have your glasses?" I say as soon as Maths is over.

"My glasses? What for?"

"Hand them over!" I command.

He gives me his glasses and squints at me. I polish the lenses on my T-shirt. I've been wanting to

---

report – Zeugnis

do this for ages. Suddenly I notice that his eyes are different colours: the left eye is blue and the right one is brown. It looks crazy but also kind of cool.

Schmidt-Bürste strides into the room. "Good morning, class!" He doesn't sound overly happy.

His satchel crashes on to his desk and he pulls himself up to full height. "This slipper business has got to stop!" His eyes are fixed on one person: me. "I won't put up with it any more. I've had a complaint from Mr Ziegler. Apparently, four people in this classroom aren't wearing slippers."

That explains it: Ziegler has given him a hard time because of me.

"From now on I want to see you all in slippers. Outside of this classroom you can walk around in gumboots or socks for all I care, but in here you'll wear slippers. Rules are rules, and if any of you break them, your parents will hear about it."

"But that's not fair, sir!" Jockel grabs his glasses and gets Schmidt-Bürste in his sights. "It's tyrannical, it's –"

Our teacher doesn't let him finish. "I don't want to hear another word. Now turn to page 23 ..."

"Let him write to my parents if he wants to," says Johanna at break-time. She smiles at me in solidarity. "See if I care!"

"He can write to my parents, too!" Mona is fearless, protected by a shield of love. "I guess it's time for Jockel to quit, though."

"You've got to be kidding!" I say in surprise.

"You don't know his dad." Mona keeps glancing round for Georg. "He's seriously strict. He'd go mad if he found out."

Mona finally spots Georg and waves at him. I leave them to it. I'd rather talk to Jockel than see them cooing over each other. He smiles as I take a seat on the wall.

"Mona told me about your dad," I say, "and it's fine by me if you want to back down. We can fight in your name, you know. They want to turn us into sheep by making us wear slippers. Well, those **leather-shod shepherds** had better think again!"

"I'm not backing down. No way!" Jockel crosses his arms **determinedly**. He looks like a boxer preparing for a fight.

The caretaker turns up with a tin of white paint. He starts painting the wall.

"That's really brave of you, Jockel."

His face goes bright red.

He looks at me nervously through his polished lenses, rubs his hands on his jeans, and then it all comes out at once. "It's only because of you," he says quickly. "I mean, I didn't use to be brave. But you showed me how, and now things are different

---

leather-shod – in Lederschuhen; shepherd – Schäfer;
determined – entschlossen

because you're here. You're fantastic, and I … I …"

Jockel suddenly **dries up**. He leans forwards and kisses me. I stare at his closed eyelids, see the caretaker painting the wall and spot Mona holding hands with Georg. I close my eyes and let it happen.

---

to dry up – still sein, verstummen

Nothing But Stars

The stage is set. Our big day has come.

The Rocky Horror Picture Show, as performed by the pupils of Ludwig-Thoma-School – better than the movie!

Georg and I get everything ready to make the scene changes easier. There won't be time for mistakes and the **transitions** have to be **slick**. The first scene takes place in front of the church.

Georg is in a bad mood. He works with grim determination and hasn't said a word. I put it down to the pressure although it wouldn't hurt to **acknowledge** my presence. He hasn't talked to me for days – not since I started seeing Jockel.

Maybe I shouldn't be going out with Jockel. We've been together since we kissed. I guess that makes him my boyfriend. There isn't a sweeter guy on the planet. He'd do anything for me and that's no exaggeration. The first day he took me home on his bicycle. It was pouring with rain, it's a long

---

transition – Übergang; slick – glatt;
to acknowledge – anerkennen

way, and I'm not especially light. But Jockel wouldn't admit defeat. He pedalled with all his heart and kept turning round to smile at me. Of course, he couldn't see anything out of his glasses – this time because of the rain. I guess he's used to cloudy vision and he managed not to crash. We were both soaking wet by the time he dropped me off, and I gave him a kiss to say thank-you.

"There's one thing I'd like to know." I had to pull away from him or he would never have stopped kissing me. "How did you do all that stuff without getting caught?"

Jockel blinked at me. He tried to look surprised.

"What about the cow? And the heart on Joe's seat?"

Jockel took off his glasses. His brown and blue eyes twinkled. "It's a **trade secret**," he said.

Then he kissed me again, and it wasn't bad, it really wasn't. But my heart didn't flutter and I couldn't help thinking of Georg. He only had to touch me and I felt totally **electrified**. I focused on Jockel to push him out of my mind.

It's been a nightmare with Georg ever since. He **avoids** me, refuses to look me in the eye, and works silently in a corner. What's his problem? I thought he was supposed to be dating Mona? He

---

trade secret – Berufsgeheimnis; electrified – elektrisiert; to avoid – aus dem Weg gehen

can't be offended because I'm seeing someone else. He's just being weird. I decide to work in silence, too.

A few days ago we were looking for an electric carving knife for the scene in which Eddie gets eaten. Jockel borrowed one from home without permission but Georg didn't want to take it. He refused **point blank**. Jockel was already in enough trouble about the slippers. It was really nice of him to pinch a knife for us, too.

Our parents had been sent a letter from school. It said something about breaking the rules by refusing to wear slippers. "Why don't you wear the damn things?" Dad demanded.

"Our teachers don't wear slippers," I explained.

"That's different."

"Is it?"

Dad gave a sigh. "God knows," he said.

He didn't mention it again. Poor Jockel wasn't so lucky. His dad wouldn't let him out of the house for a week. There were other punishments, too, but Jockel wouldn't really talk about it. He was his usual happy self – madly in love and determined not to wear slippers.

Georg is setting up the stage. I walk round and put bags of rice on the chairs. It was my idea. We want the atmosphere to be like the cinema in Mu-

---

point blank – geradeheraus, direkt

nich, with the audience throwing rice and singing along to the music.

"Hi there!" Jockel appears in the doorway. His glasses are clean and his eyes are twinkling. "Fancy a break? We could get a hot chocolate." He rattles the change in his pocket to show **it's his treat**. I kiss him on the cheek. I could do with a break. Georg and I are nearly done.

"I'm afraid she's busy."

Excuse me? Since when has Georg made my decisions?

"Uh, I was talking to Annika." Jockel looks surprised. "Anyway, a little break won't hurt."

"For your information, Jockel, we're actually really busy. We've got masses to do. We'll be lucky if we make it." Three sentences in a row – that must be a record for Georg.

Jockel steps forwards with his hands on his hips. "So you think you can **boss** everyone **around**, do you? You may have painted a few **props** but –"

At that moment Mona walks in. She leans over to kiss Georg. "Not now!" he snaps. "This joker is trying to tell us what to do!"

Mona **freezes** in surprise. Jockel and Georg square up to each other. No one cares whether *I*

It's his treat. – Es geht auf seine Rechnung.; to boss around – herumkommandieren; props – Requisiten; to freeze – erstarren

want a break or not. I decide to have a hot chocolate with Mona. They can fight it out if they want. It's got nothing to do with me.

"I can't wait for the show to be over," says Mona. She blows on her hot chocolate. "Then Georg will be his old self again and not a stressed-out zombie."

I stir my hot chocolate and hope everything will be fine. I make a new wish for every **turn** of the spoon. Everything will be fine ... Whatever "fine" means. I don't really believe it, though. I've got a strange feeling that the dark cloud hanging over Georg's head is about to burst all over us.

"Has Alex been in touch?"

I shake my head. Of course not. Why would he? It's over. He finished with me, and now I've got Jockel.

"Georg keeps asking about him." Mona looks at me.

She's got to be kidding.

"He talks about Alex almost every day."

Unbelievable. Why would Georg want to hear about Alex? I give my head a little shake as if everything will fall into place. Then I **gulp down** my hot chocolate and run. Mona stays behind and I

---

turn – Umdrehung;
to gulp down – (Essen, Trinken) hinunterstürzen, verschlingen

ask Jockel to keep her company. He looks all right, so I guess he and Georg didn't actually fight. Either way, I've had my break, so he'll have to **make do with** Mona.

Two hours later the moment of truth has come. Every last seat is taken. There's room for 300 people – 350 if you really **cram** them **in**. Everyone's chatting, taking off their raincoats, saving seats for their friends. Georg and I are ready, of course. We even had time to spare. My parents are here – well, they had to come, really.

Benno and Christian have disguised themselves as **hunchbacked ghouls** with blood dripping out of their mouths. Actually, it's too **garish** to be blood. Georg waves at a middle-aged couple sitting shyly at the back. His parents have dressed up for the occasion.

The headmaster appears in front of the curtain and gives a speech. I spot Mona in the audience but I can't see Jockel. Someone **tugs** on my T-shirt. I turn round and see Johanna in her Janet outfit. She looks white as a sheet and is trembling all over. "I can't go through with this, Annika," she whispers **miserably**.

---

to make do with – vorliebnehmen mit;
to cram in – vollstopfen;
hunchbacked ghoul – bucklige Horrorgestalt;
garish – grell; to tug – zupfen; miserable – jämmerlich

I go backstage with her. "What's wrong?"

Tears pour down her cheeks as she points to her throat. "It's my voice … It's gone!"

This can't be happening! Has the whole village gone mad?

"You'll be fine, Johanna. It's just the excitement. Try not to panic." I give her a little shake, which doesn't seem to help. "There's no need to be scared of the audience – they're people with bodily functions just like us." What a dumb comment. It's the kind of thing my dad would say. Why should Johanna stop worrying because the audience has bodily functions? She looks at me **in bewilderment**. I **embrace** her and give her a little squeeze. "You'll be fine. I know you can do it!"

"… so sit back and enjoy yourselves!" The headmaster has finished his speech. No one was listening but most people heard the last line. Thunderous applause. We're on!

I leave Johanna by the stage door and try not to notice how miserable she is. I run back to Georg. "OK?"

He nods. The lights go out and the stage is illuminated. Georg is about to lift the curtain but Jockel runs on to the stage. He waves an enormous sign: SAY NO TO SLIPPERS! "Sorry, **folks**, but I just

---

in bewilderment – verwirrt; to embrace – umarmen; folks – Leute

wanted to take the opportunity to say a few words."

"Jockel!" I hiss, trying to keep my voice down. "What the hell are you doing?" He smiles reassuringly. The room falls silent.

"As some of you know, the pupils in this school are **obliged** to wear slippers. If it weren't for Annika" – Jockel points at me and I die of embarrassment – "we wouldn't have thought to object. My girlfriend has opened our eyes to this **indignity**. Why should we be forced to wear slippers when our teachers wear shoes?"

Some of our classmates whistle in appreciation.

"Since then a group of us have refused to wear slippers. We've been punished by our teacher" – Jockel signals for Mr Schmidt-Bürste to stand up – "who has the pleasure of wearing ordinary shoes."

Everyone stares at our Latin teacher. He gets to his feet, glances round the room, takes off one shoe and holds it up for everyone to see: it's a great big fluffy tiger paw. A slipper. Everyone talks excitedly to their neighbours and Jockel loses his thread. This isn't something he'd prepared for. Schmidt-Bürste has shocked him into silence.

"Uh ... I mean ... Well, it's obviously a trick ..."

---

to be obliged to do sth – etwas tun müssen;
indignity – Demütigung

Georg **digs** me in the ribs. "Do something!"

I creep on to the stage and pull Jockel away from the spotlight. Schmidt-Bürste replaces his slipper in satisfaction and sits back down.

"But Annika, we can't let him wear slippers! What are we going to do?" Jockel is **outraged**.

"Sit down next to Mona. We'll talk later."

Jockel looks at me in despair. I get rid of him with a kiss on the cheek and he trots off with his **placard**.

The curtain rises. Brad and Janet come running out of the church and everyone claps and screams. OK, Johanna, start singing. I know you can do it. I **cross my fingers** and wish with all my **might**. The music has started. It's her cue. Sing Johanna! She glances at me. I shake my fist in her direction. Sing! She sings. Her voice isn't hoarse or croaky. It's as strong and clear as ever. I lower my head in **relief** and **exhale**. It feels as though I haven't breathed for hours.

"Good job you're here," Georg whispers. I feel his eyes pierce my heart. I turn round and blush. Thank God the song is nearly over and we have to start work. Everything goes to plan. We've prac-

---

to dig – *hier:* stoßen; outraged – empört;
placard – Plakat, Transparent;
to cross one's fingers – die Daumen drücken;
might – Kraft; relief – Erleichterung;
to exhale – ausatmen

tised a hundred times and we know exactly what to do. The audience claps wildly as the castle rises out of the mist. They seem to love the elevator. Georg smiles at me. He isn't tense any more. Somehow I felt more comfortable with his anger. Now I don't know what to do. I just smile.

We get to the finale and the castle zooms through space. The ghouls are on their way to Planet Transexual in the galaxy of Transylvania. Georg and I pull the castle up to the ceiling from above. The smoke machine churns out mist and the audience goes wild. Smiling, the actors come forwards to take their hundredth bow. Johanna wants to say something: "And special thanks to Georg and Annika who made our fantastic set."

She points up at us and everyone raises their hands in applause. Mona and Jockel are on their chairs, **whooping** and yelling. We wave down, grinning from ear to ear.

After a while everyone pulls on their jackets and gets ready to go. The curtain falls and it's over. Georg and I sit for a moment, basking in our success.

"It's good to see you happy again," I say to Georg. "Everyone loved it."

Georg gazes into the distance. "That's not why I'm smiling. I've made a decision, Annika."

---

to whoop – schreien

Somehow I get the feeling that his decision has something to do with me. My eye starts twitching. I thought that was Mum's speciality! "Hadn't we better go down and join the others?" I hold my eyelid down with one finger. I start to leave but Georg pulls me back.

"I've decided to be honest with you. I want you to know how I feel. I've been in love with you since the day I first saw you with your sketchpad."

I almost **choke**. I feel as though I'm **running out of oxygen**. "But you're dating Mona."

"I know. It was a mistake. It should never have happened."

"Things don't just happen."

"Well, how come you're with Jockel? You can't say you're suited to each other either. I bet that just happened, too." He looks into my eyes and sees that I feel the same way. I've let myself get into a relationship because the person I love is dating someone else. I try to look away but my eyes won't let me.

"I tried to tell you before," he says, "that's why I wanted to show you the devil's rocks. But then I heard about Alex and ..."

Georg kisses me, and I realize that you don't need oxygen to kiss. It doesn't matter that I've

---

to choke – ersticken;
to run out of oxygen – die Luft ausgehen

stopped breathing. I've never been kissed like this before. It's an **indescribable** feeling. All of a sudden, I've forgotten about everything else and the world explodes into a million tiny stars. Nothing but stars.

---

indescribable – unbeschreiblich

The Decent Thing

23.53: The **digits** on my alarm clock glow in the dark. I've been lying in bed for ages but I'm still wide awake. Normally I think of something boring and it sends me to sleep, but tonight I can't stop thinking of Georg. I concentrate on imagining Hannchen and Helga. They're **strutting around** the garden, **pecking** at the ground. Then Georg pops into the picture. I remember how he kissed me, and my heart starts racing while my mind **churns** like a crazy machine. Georg, Mona, Jockel and me. Why does it have to be so complicated?

Georg and I kissed and kissed and kissed, then all of a sudden, the millions of tiny stars turned back to normal life. I opened my eyes and pulled away from him. "We can't do this. It's not fair on Mona and Jockel."

I grabbed my things and ran off.

"Wait!" Georg shouted after me. I didn't even

---

decent – anständig; digit – Ziffer;
to strut around – herumstolzieren; to peck – picken;
to churn – *hier:* rattern

turn round. I had to get out of there before I changed my mind.

I raced down the stairs and almost crashed into Mona and Jockel. "We were coming to get your autograph," said Jockel, looking at me proudly.

I started to panic. Surely they could see what had happened? I felt as though it was written in big flashing letters on my head: I KISSED GEORG.

It wouldn't take long for them to notice that something was up. I needed an exit strategy and fast.

"Sorry," I murmured. "I'm not feeling too good." I hurried down the stairs and out of the building. I was safe for now, but what the hell was I supposed to do next?

I thought about running away. Eventually I'd forget about Georg and I'd never see Mona again. If I stayed, I'd have to be nice to her and feel like a **traitor**. If I left, she and Jockel would never know what happened. I'd be gone.

23.55: I stare at my alarm clock and listen to the **shutters** rattling in the wind. A door squeaks as though someone is opening it slowly. You hear all kinds of weird noises when it's stormy outside. I roll on to my back and look at the ceiling. The trees **cast** their shadow through my window and dance wildly on the walls.

---

traitor – Verräter/-in; shutter – Fensterladen;
to cast – werfen

I can't run away. I don't want to take the **coward's** way out. I have to face the situation **head-on**, and that means breaking up with Jockel. It's time to do the decent thing. Kissing Georg was **proof** that Jockel and I aren't meant for each other. We can't be together, but how am I supposed to explain that to him? It's not like with Alex. It's hard splitting up with someone who's sweet and nice and unbelievably kind.

I hear a **rustling** noise. I freeze and listen **intently** in the darkness. Silence. Then I hear it again. I feel for the light switch and flood my room with light. It's just a mouse. It probably paid a visit to Guinea Pig and got bored. It can't be much fun spending time with a cloudy-eyed overgrown mouse with depressive tendencies. The mouse **scampers** across the floor, pushes its way under the door and disappears into the hall.

I turn off the light, relieved that it was only a mouse. I glance at my alarm clock: 23.58. A new day starts in two more minutes – a day in which I'll have to **dump** Jockel. It's no use putting it off.

Hopefully he'll be cool about it. Maybe he'll say, "Don't worry, Annika. It was great while it lasted

---

coward – Feigling; head-on – frontal, direkt;
proof – Beweis; rustling – Rascheln;
intent – *hier:* angestrengt;
to scamper – huschen;
to dump – Schluss machen mit

and I'll never forget you. But some things just aren't meant to be."

Maybe we can stay friends and start another protest movement. We could join forces against white walls or nicotine-**stained** bus drivers or something.

I smile to myself in the darkness. Then doubts start to creep in. There's no knowing how he might react. What if he's mad at me and starts screaming? He could turn the whole class against me. He might burst into tears and beg me not to break up with him. I'd have to look into his eyes – one blue and one brown, both filled with tears. That would be worse.

I hear footsteps. They're coming from upstairs. I sit up with a **jolt**, hold my breath and listen. There's someone up there.

The digits roll over again: 00.00. The church bells **chime** midnight. It's **witching hour** ...

I know for a fact that there's a ghost out there. I get **goose bumps** at the thought of it. I bet the farmer who used to live here was abandoned by his lover. She left him for another man. He waited for her, day in, day out, but the months and years went by and she never came back. Now his ghost

---

stained – fleckig; jolt – Ruck; to chime – läuten;
witching hour – Geisterstunde;
goose bumps – Gänsehaut

is waiting, still longing to hold her in his arms. I **flip the light switch** but the room stays dark. The digits on my alarm clock have disappeared. It must be a **power cut**. We're always having power cuts, but this is the worst possible moment for the lights to go out. I picture a ghost with laser-like eyes burning through our power lines.

The room is pitch black without the red glow from my alarm clock. The noises are even louder than before. The wind **howls** around the house, filling it with rustling, scratching and groaning sounds. Maybe an army of ghosts is **invading**. I hear footsteps again. This time they're right outside my door.

"Listen! I'm sure there's something there ..."

Phew! It's only Dad. I climb out of bed, feel my way to the door and open it. He's standing in the corridor, holding a candle and arguing with Mum.

"What kind of something?" comes her voice from the bedroom.

"How should I know? **Burglars**, maybe," whispers Dad.

"Burglars? Have you seen the state of this place? No one's that stupid," Mum hisses.

Dad doesn't listen. He's determined to **invest-**

---

to flip the light switch – das Licht anknipsen;
power cut – Stromausfall; to howl – heulen;
to invade – eindringen; burglar – Einbrecher/-in;
to investigate – untersuchen

igate. I go, too. **Inquisitiveness** isn't always a good thing and I probably got it from him.

We creep up the wooden staircase. The first floor is still uninhabitable. We hear all kinds of noises – not just creaks and groans but drips as well. Drip, drip, drip. The roof hasn't been repaired and rain **seeps** through the tarpaulin as it shakes in the wind. The clouds part for a second and the hall is lit with milky moonlight. It feels spooky, like we're walking into the silvery **strands** of a spider's web. The **faint** glow of Dad's candle illuminates the room that will one day be my bedroom – if I haven't left home by the time that it's ready. I bet this is where the farmer used to stand and wait for his lover. A shiver runs down my spine. I keep close to Dad while we investigate the other rooms. Suddenly I spot two shadows in the darkness. They look like people, small people, people like …

"Benno?" I say, surprised.

"Shush." The voice comes from the shadow. It's Benno. Benno and Christian. "We're looking for **bats**."

"For *what*?" growls Dad.

I glance round the room. It's true – there are bats hanging from the **beams**. I'm not sure whether to

---

inquisitiveness – Wissbegierde, Neugier;
to seep – sickern; strand – *hier:* Faden; faint – schwach;
bat – Fledermaus; beam – Dachbalken

feel relieved or alarmed. What if the farmer has turned into a vampire and is hanging upside down in our rickety old house, waiting to **feast on** our souls in revenge for his lover's **betrayal**?

"We're looking for bats," Benno says patiently.

"At this time of night?" Dad sounds **cross**. Then he screams in pain and starts hopping around like a **lunatic**. He must have trodden on a nail.

Either way, it puts an end to Benno's nature lesson. The bats fly off in terror and Dad sends Benno and Christian to bed.

"Don't let me catch you up here again," he shouts angrily. A few minutes later he's grimacing with pain as Mum puts **iodine** on his cut.

"At least Benno is taking an interest in nature. I thought that was the idea," I say, trying to get a reaction.

"Not in the middle of the night!"

"Maybe you should give him back his Game Boy," I suggest with a grin.

"Over my dead body!" Dad folds his arms determinedly. I guess he means it.

I shrug and take myself back to bed. Let Dad figure out how to deal with Benno by himself. I've got problems of my own. I don't want Jockel to

---

to feast on – sich gütlich tun an; betrayal – Verrat;
cross – sauer; lunatic – Wahnsinnige/-r;
iodine – Jod

turn into a **restless** ghost or a bloodthirsty vampire. I want him to get over me. My throat **tightens**. Then it hits me – I could write to him instead. By the time I speak to him he'll be able to talk about it calmly. I decide to write a letter. Seconds later I'm asleep.

The next morning I march to the postbox. The streets have been decorated for the annual village fête, and the trees are **festooned** with blue-and-white **ribbons**. When I get to the postbox, I stop and turn the letter over in my hands. It took three hours to write. I had to start again and again until I was satisfied with the result. The first section is about how much Jockel means to me and how great it was to have his friendship from the start. After that I go on to say that we're not really right for each other. Sure, I don't expect him to like what I say, but there's no other way. I've got to break up with him. I post the letter.

The envelope **thuds down** on to the pile of letters in the box and I notice something **odd**. The bus stop has been decorated, too. But instead of the usual blue-and-white colour scheme, the rib-

---

restless – rastlos, ruhelos;
to tighten – sich zuschnüren;
to festoon – verzieren; ribbon – Band;
to thud down – mit einem dumpfen Ton fallen;
odd – merkwürdig

bons are red. The whole bus shelter is **draped with** red ribbons and artificial roses. A red cardboard heart **dangles** from the roof. It says: *Annika, you're a star!*

My eyes fill with tears. I feel terrible. Jockel makes all these amazing gestures, and how do I thank him? I dump him by letter. It's cowardly, **mean** and **wretched**. Jockel doesn't deserve this kind of treatment. If I'm going to break up with him, I should look him in the eye and tell him in person. It's not fair to send a letter. I roll up my sleeve, squeeze my arm through the **slot** and fish around for the envelope. I grab a handful of mail. Hopefully my letter is in there somewhere, too. I try to pull out my hand but it's stuck. No matter what I do, I can't get my elbow out of the slot. This can't be happening. It went in OK, so it's got to come out. I start sweating. A farmer drives past in his tractor and I feel my heart racing like crazy. He stares at me open-mouthed, and I give him a friendly smile as though it's normal for people to have their arms in postboxes. I use my spare hand to wave. He waves back in astonishment and shakes his head. As soon as he's out of sight, I try pulling and twisting as hard as I can, but it's hope-

---

to be draped with – geschmückt sein mit;
to dangle – baumeln; mean – gemein;
wretched – erbärmlich; slot – Schlitz

less. My arm is so happy in the postbox that it refuses to come out. It reminds me of the night that Georg the calf was born.

"Feeling better now?"

I turn round in horror. Mona has appeared out of nowhere. That's all I need.

"I, uh, posted the wrong letter," I stutter. I don't want everyone knowing I'm a coward. "And now my arm is stuck."

Mona grins. "Reminds me of when you delivered Georg the calf."

I groan and roll my eyes.

"Hang on, I'll help." Mona rummages in her handbag. I mean, who would have thought Mona would ever have a handbag? She pulls out a tube of hand cream (!) and covers my arm in **moisturiser**.

"Now try again," she encourages me. Seconds later my arm slips out of the slot and I'm free.

"Thanks," I say, hoping to God that I've pulled out Jockel's letter. I flip through the envelopes. Phew. "Here it is."

I wave it hastily, then stuff it in my jeans pocket. I put the other letters back in the box.

"What was wrong with you last night?" Mona looks at me intently and I feel a pang of conscience.

---

moisturiser – Feuchtigkeitscreme

"Er, I'm not sure. I just felt sick. It came on really quickly," I lie.

"Poor you. Georg came down with it, too."

Oh really? So Georg **faked** illness, too ... "Must be going round, I guess. Maybe it was all the excitement."

Mona nods. "Want to go shopping?"

"What, now?"

Mona nods again. I don't feel like shopping, and anyway, there aren't any cool shops round here. Besides, I don't want to spend time with Mona in case she notices something. What if she guesses that I kissed her boyfriend? What if she can tell that I wouldn't mind kissing him again and again and again ...

"Mum asked me to help in the garden," I say, rolling my eyes theatrically. "I'm supposed to scare away the slugs. And Rocky needs a walk."

"Oh well, some other time," says Mona.

A few minutes later I'm sitting cross-legged on the bed, staring at the telephone. I can practically hear it talking to me. It's telling me what to do. "Go on then," it orders me, "call him. Dial his number, fix a meeting, arrange to see him now. For God's sake, Annika, just do it!"

I pull myself together and call. I'm NOT a

---

to fake – vortäuschen

coward. No, seriously, I'm not! It rings four times, then five, six ... Maybe he's busy. Seven, eight, nine ... He could be out. Ten, eleven ... What if –

"Hi!"

"Hey, Jockel, it's Annika."

"Cool! I was just going to call you. How are you feeling? You looked awful last night, really pale."

"Oh, I'm fine," I say, pulling nervously on my duvet. Go ahead and tell him, I order myself.

Jockel is chatting cheerfully about something else. "I can't believe what he did. I never imagined Schmidt-Bürste could **pull a stunt** like that. We can't let him get away with it."

"I don't see why not. It was a pretty **gutsy** thing to do. Gutsy and smart. He deserves a pat on the back, if you ask me. Now we're all sheep together, even him."

Jockel falls silent. He must be thinking it over and making up his mind. Then he baas like a sheep: "Baa, baa!" I can't help laughing.

Annika, you've got to tell him!

Jockel is serious again. "If we're all going to wear slippers, you'll have to get a pair, too. How about now?"

"Now?" I give my duvet a sharp tug. I think about it. Why not meet up with him now? I called

---

to pull a stunt – eine Nummer abziehen;
gutsy – mutig

because I wanted to speak to him face-to-face. I should go shopping with him, then end it.

"Uh, I'm busy right now," I hear myself saying. "I've got to, uh, help out in the garden. And tomorrow I'm busy, too. I'm really busy in general. But thanks for the bus shelter. I mean, for the hearts and the roses and everything. It was really sweet of you. Really sweet, but right now I've ..." My **nostrils** twitch. I can smell something. It stinks around here. "Sorry, Jockel, I've got to go. I think our toilet has just exploded."

"Your toilet?"

"Bye!"

I ring off and throw the handset on to the bed. I can't go shopping for slippers and pretend everything is fine when really I'm about to break up with him. I should wait until Monday. Although ... The smell creeps under my door and **wafts** towards me like a cloud of black smoke. What the hell is that? It's disgusting! I hold my nose and run into the hall. The smell gets worse but at least I can see where it's coming from: Benno, a walking source of smell pollution. He looks as though he's fallen head-first into a **septic tank**.

"... and then I fell in." Benno smiles. Not even

---

nostril – Nasenloch; to waft – schweben;
septic tank – Jauchegrube

an unexpected swim in a pool of cow dung can shake him up.

"Are you out of your mind?" Mum drags him into the bathroom. "God knows what could have happened to you!"

"What?" Benno climbs calmly into the bath.

"You could have **drowned**." Dad decides to join in. "You wouldn't be the first, you know."

"We all have to die some time," says Benno.

"Not in a septic tank, we don't!" Mum directs a jet of cold water towards him. The water doesn't look much cleaner than the dung.

Dad gives a little cough, clears his throat, coughs and clears his throat again. "Uh, look here, Benno, I've been thinking. What would you say if we gave you back your Game Boy?"

I smile to myself. Is he serious?

Dad sees that I'm grinning and looks embarrassed. He picks up a towel, folds it, puts it back on the shelf and lays it flat.

"Oh, that old **pile of junk**," says Benno. "You can keep it."

Dad frowns. This isn't the reaction he'd expected.

"It's no use to anyone." Benno turns round for Mum to wash his back. "The new ones are much better. There's one that –"

---

to drown – ertrinken; pile of junk – Haufen Müll

"Forget it!" Dad interrupts.

I leave the three of them and take Rocky for a walk. We wander over fields and meadows until we come to a bench by the **stream**. Rocky runs around sniffing at stuff and I sit down with my sketchpad. Drawing is always the best way of clearing my head and thinking of nothing. I decide to call the picture "Two Ducks By a Stream". I start sketching and feel calmer right away. I look at the outline of the **drake** and suddenly it occurs to me: ducks stay with their partners for life. Lucky them! I put away my sketchpad in irritation and whistle for Rocky.

We walk home and I spot Jockel at the door with Mum. What's he saying to her? Didn't I tell him I was busy? I'm about to crouch behind a bush and wait until he's gone when Rocky pulls away from me and **dashes over** to Mum. Tail wagging, he turns round and fetches me home.

Thanks a million, Rocky.

"I know you're busy right now," says Jockel, "but I have to tell you something."

Mum takes the stupid dog and vanishes inside.

What does Jockel want to tell me? I thought I was the one who had something to say ... I lean up against the wall and look him in the eye. "What is it?"

---

stream – Bach; drake – Erpel; to dash over – hinrennen

He **wrings his hands** and looks kind of pale. "You know the stuff about the bus shelter and everything – the hearts and the messages and all that … Well, the thing is, it wasn't me."

"What?" I stare at Jockel **in disbelief**. That was the last thing I expected to hear.

"I know you're going to be mad at me and I'm sorry. I wanted to tell you right away but I didn't dare."

"Who was it then?" I ask him, shocked.

Jockel shrugs. "God knows."

Jockel has made his confession, so I **summon** the courage to make mine. "I need to tell you something, too." Now it's my turn to wring my hands.

"I know what you're going to say. You want to break up with me." Jockel is full of surprises. "You like Georg and he likes you. Right?"

"How did you find out?"

Jockel shrugs again and looks at his feet. "It's just a feeling, I guess."

For a moment I'm **floored**. Who would have thought a guy would guess a thing like that? He must be really sensitive. Isn't that what everyone wants? A man who's in touch with his feelings. But

---

to wring one's hands – die Hände ringen;
in disbelief – ungläubig;
to summon – *hier:* (Mut) zusammennehmen;
to be floored – verblüfft

I don't want Jockel. There's nothing I can do about it. There isn't any **spark**. "I'm sorry," I say, and I mean it.

"You can kiss pretty well, you know." Jockel manages a smile. "I guess it's just not meant to be."

He smiles again and walks away.

I catch the afternoon bus to the local metropolis – our school, a high street and some houses. I take Benno and Christian with me. They're looking for brand new Game Boys. Poor Dad will have to pay the bill.

I go to the shoe shop and buy the ugliest slippers I can find: brown cord with a decorative gold **clasp**. If Georg sees me wearing them, he'll run straight back to Mona. At least her slippers are just old-fashioned instead of **downright** unattractive.

After our shopping trip the bus drops us off in Höllenhausen and I stop to look at the bus shelter. *Annika, you're a star!* If only my admirer knew.

---

spark – Fünkchen; clasp – Schnalle;
downright – ausgesprochen

Update
from the Village Front

Countryside correspondent Annika Weber with all the latest news ...

Here in the rain capital of the world a transformation is taking place. Contrary to all expectations (including mine) the Weber family's "jewel", a **dilapidated** wreck of a building, is turning into a habitable house. Incredibly, Mrs Weber, a woman of almost infinite patience and charity, is responsible for the change.

The stress was too great. One morning the muddy brown drinking water contained floating particles of an unidentifiable substance. Mrs Weber drank a glass and collapsed minutes later while milking the cow. She narrowly escaped being kicked to death, then almost died of **suffocation** when the cow lay down beside her. It was **the last straw.**

It was another wet day in Höllenhausen, but Mrs Weber marched outside and **trudged** through her organic vegetable patch, ignoring the hun-

---

dilapidated – baufällig; suffocation – Ersticken;
the last straw – der letzte Tropfen;
to trudge – stampfen

dreds of baby slugs that had appeared there overnight. She headed straight for the chicken pen. Helga and Hannchen had never succeeded in producing a chick. Mrs Weber grabbed some eggs and scrambled them for breakfast. She served them up to her husband with an ultimatum:

"Join the shooting club today or I'm getting a divorce."

Mr Weber choked on his breakfast and **spattered** his daughter with egg.

"Let me know what you decide," said Mrs Weber darkly. She got up, went outside, **untethered** the cow and walked it up the hill to Mona's mum. Then she abandoned her environmental principles and went shopping for **slug pellets** and insecticides. Her vegetable patch is no longer an "organic" garden. She bought a tray of new plants. Her final purchase was a cute female guinea pig that she **christened** Guinea Pigette. Her last reserves of rage were used to chop down the "poor old" outhouse. She used the wood to build a state-of-the-art guinea pig run. Her husband **skulked back** from the village, holding his membership certificate at arm's length. She greeted him with a military salute.

---

to spatter – bespritzen; to untether – losbinden;
slug pellets – Schneckenkorn; to christen – taufen;
to skulk back – zurückschleichen

The annual village fête took place that weekend. Mrs Weber generously donated three home-baked cakes and won the **support** of the village ladies. The war veterans' association **conducted** its memorial service at quarter to four in the morning. Everyone including Hermann awoke to the sound of gunfire. It was a bad start to the day for Mr Weber, but he couldn't go back to sleep. As the rifle club's newest member, he was obliged to take part in the shooting contest. The villagers were curious to see how the "city boy" would do. Mr Weber hated making a fool of himself. He spent most of the morning drinking large amounts of beer. He had never touched a weapon, let alone fired one.

Things got worse when he heard about the **consolation** prize: "Sepp Meier will teach the loser how to shoot!"

Mr Weber drank two more beers.

At last it was his turn to shoot. He closed his eyes, took aim, and hit the centre of the target – a **bullseye**! Mr Weber had won the contest.

In spite of his pacifist beliefs Mr Weber put his trophy on display in the kitchen. His bullseye had other, more **startling**, results. All of a sudden,

---

support – Unterstützung; to conduct – durchführen;
consolation – Trost; bullseye – Volltreffer;
startling – überraschend

the builder found he had time for the roof. If it suited Mr Weber, he could start the next day. Soon afterwards the plumber appeared at the door. He couldn't work out why the Webers' bill had been so high. He must have made a mistake. Anyone would think the pipes were made of gold! To make up for the inconvenience, he was willing to finish the job and forget about the cost. If it was all right with Mr Weber, he could start the next day …

At last, months after their arrival, the Webers are at peace. Benno Weber and his new friend Christian are playing on their Game Boys in their tree house. Annika Weber is looking forward to throwing a party in her room on the first floor. Mr Weber is proudly inspecting his trophy and Mrs Weber is keeping an eye on the cockerel. Hermann hasn't crowed since the early-morning gunfire.

You've been listening to Annika Weber, reporting live from the countryside at the heart of the action.

No Matter What

"Happy birthday to you, happy birthday to you, happy ... " My parents are standing in my spacious new bedroom, beneath my brand new **watertight** ceiling, holding a birthday cake complete with candles. They're in their pyjamas and so is Benno. He doesn't usually get up this early, but family traditions are **sacred**. We'll always celebrate each other's birthdays, no matter what.

I take a deep breath and blow out the candles. Rocky **wolfs down** the cake. It's time for me to make a wish. I can't make up my mind. Should I wish for the party to work out? Or for Georg to turn up, too?

Georg has been off school since we kissed. Not even Mona, who's supposed to be his girlfriend, has seen him. At first I thought he was pretending. *How pathetic!* I thought. Staying in bed just so he doesn't have to face Mona ... So I called him. I wanted to make him feel as small and

---

watertight – wasserdicht;
sacred – heilig; to wolf down – verschlingen

insignificant as one of Mum's slugs. I rang him to give him a good dose of slug pellets and finish him off **for good**. I couldn't believe that he hadn't bothered to phone Mona.

The truth was, Georg had the flu. His **tonsils** were swollen and he couldn't even speak. He couldn't do anything. It took me ages to catch on.

"Georg, is that you?"

"Huhhhhh ..."

"It's me, Annika."

I heard breathing.

"Georg, why haven't you called Mona? It's the least you could do ..." If only I'd realized. He couldn't call Mona because he couldn't say a thing.

"Uhhhhh."

"Georg?"

His dad grabbed the phone. "Hello, there! Sorry, but Georg has lost his voice. The doctor told him not to speak. Hang on, he's writing a note ... Wait a minute ... It says: *It was amazing.*"

I **cleared the call** and dropped the handset like a hot potato. That wasn't why I'd phoned. I'd been worried about Mona. I could feel my heart fluttering. And I hadn't even spoken to Georg, just his dad.

---

insignificant – unbedeutend; for good – endgültig; tonsils – Mandeln; to clear the call – auflegen

I think about my birthday wish. Georg is ill, so there's no point wishing for him to be at the party. And anyway, it wouldn't do any good. No, I'm going to wish for everything to be right between him and Mona. That's what I want, isn't it?

I leap out of bed to stop myself thinking about it. I wish for breakfast and get it right away. That's the joy of birthday wishes – they have a magic of their own.

I spend the rest of the day preparing my room for the party. Dad finds an ancient set of disco lights – red, green and blue. He fixes them to my newly painted ceiling. Meanwhile, Mum dashes about in the kitchen. Sausages are boiling, burgers are sizzling, the mustard is in pots ... The whole house stinks like a **chip shop**. The party is my birthday present and Mum and Dad want it to be a success. Benno has been **dispatched** to Christian's house. My parents are spending the night in Munich by themselves.

"I can't wait to see Munich," Mum sighs. Her love affair with the countryside is definitely over.

As soon as they've gone, I turn on the shower and stand in the jet of crystal-clear water. Mona arrives with a salad. "I'll leave it in the kitchen," she yells through the door. I turn down the temperature until I'm freezing cold.

---

chip shop – Pommesbude; to dispatch – wegschicken

Mona was really grateful when I told her that I'd spoken to Georg. "How sweet of you to call him for me. You're a real friend, you know, Annika."

The trouble is, Mona had been trying to call him, too. She only wanted to find out how he was and if there was anything she could do. But Georg's parents wouldn't let her speak to him. "Georg can't talk to anyone. The doctor said no phone calls and no visits. He's got a nasty case of **flu**."

I tried to reassure her. "He sounded really sick. He couldn't say a word."

Mona didn't seem convinced. "Then why did they let you talk to him and not me? I wouldn't have minded if he couldn't speak. The sound of my voice might have helped."

Mona tried to smile. People know in their heart of hearts when things aren't right. They just **fob** themselves **off** with ridiculous explanations and don't admit it to themselves. When the truth comes out, they realize that they've known it all along.

It didn't take me long to realize that something wasn't right with Alex and Suse. I knew Alex hadn't called me for ages and that Suse hadn't mentioned Robbie for a while. I'd guessed the truth before I burst through the door and caught

---

flu – Grippe; to fob sb off – jmdn. abspeisen

the two of them kissing. If I'd listened to my instincts, I would have saved myself a lot of pain.

Why hadn't Suse told me?

I looked at Mona. She was waiting for me to speak. I had to tell her the truth before things got any worse.

"Maybe his dad thought I was you," I suggested. *You coward*, I told myself.

Mona smiled. "I guess so. It was probably just a mistake."

I'm still standing in the shower. I turn off the water and wait. I can't bring myself to get out.

"Come on, Annika!" Mona pokes her head around the door. She's holding a burger. "Wow, these things taste great. If you don't hurry up, everyone will be here and you'll still be in the shower!"

I couldn't wish for a better friend than Mona. I promise myself that I'll tell her everything as soon as the party is over. I can't go on like this, pretending things are OK. Besides, Georg will break up with Mona as soon as he can talk. He's too honest to do anything else. She'll ask why, and he'll tell her that it's because of me. I don't want him to say anything until I've spoken to her first. At least that way she'll have one less reason to hate me.

"Come on, hurry up!" Mona is in a good mood, partly because of the party and partly because she's got a friend who **sticks up for** her and the boyfriend of her dreams. Why shouldn't she be happy? Her doubts are forgotten. She can carry on as normal, just like anyone would.

I decide to do the same. It's my birthday and I want to celebrate properly. I just have time to do my special party hairstyle. I twist my hair into strands, roll them on to the top of my head and pin them in place like miniature horns.

"Hey, that looks cool." Mona likes my hair.

I plan to surprise all the village kids by wearing slippers to my party. It seems like a great idea until I see that everyone else is wearing them, too. They're all dressed in slippers, even Jockel and … Georg!

"What are you doing here?" Mona shrieks excitedly, throwing her arms around his neck. "Are you really OK?"

Georg looks at me over her shoulder. I stare back in panic and shake my head: *Don't say anything for the moment. Wait until after the party!*

Georg **disentangles** himself **from** Mona. "Happy birthday, Annika," he says hoarsely. He gives me a kiss on the cheek and a copy of *Dracula*.

"Thanks Georg, that's brilliant." I'm practically on fire.

---

to stick up for sb – für jmdn. eintreten;
to disentangle oneself from – sich befreien von

Mona grabs his arm and pulls him into the kitchen. "Come on, you should eat something. God, I can't believe how much I've missed you." Mona is determined to **claim** him for herself. Who can blame her?

Jockel prods me in the ribs. "Your face is bright red."

My mind is racing. *What the hell is Georg doing here?* What I mean is: *I'm so glad he came!* But it's the last thing I want to admit to anyone. I **grunt** something to Jockel about people with flu being better off in bed and hurry away. Everyone loves my new room. Jockel starts DJ-ing – he can't see anything through his smeared glasses but he's actually pretty good. A few people start dancing and I chat, laugh, wander round and try not to look at Georg. I can feel his eyes on me.

I can't believe how much things have changed in the space of a year. My last birthday was spent with Suse. The two of us were best friends – Robbie and Alex didn't exist for us back then. Now I've fallen out with Suse because she's dating Alex, who's my ex. I started dating Jockel but broke up with him when I fell in love with Georg. And Georg is dating my new best friend. Plus someone keeps sending me love messages.

"It won't be much of a secret if you don't quit

---

to claim for – Anspruch erheben auf; to grunt – knurren

staring," Jockel whispers. He's only trying to help. "You'd better be careful or Mona will notice."

I stop staring at Georg and peer into Jockel's cloudy glasses. "I don't know what you're talking about."

Come on, Annika, I tell myself, *you know exactly what he's talking about it!*

Jockel just raises his eyebrows. "Too late now," he says, **backing away**.

Too late? I glance at Georg and see him arguing with Mona. Her face shows a mixture of disbelief, disappointment and **fury**. It seems like a good time for me to **sneak off** and get something to eat … But Jockel was right. It's too late already. Mona marches up to me, slaps me and strides away.

"Mona!"

I want to run after her and tell her everything, but I can't think what to say. I guess this is how Suse felt, too. I hurry after her, determined to stop her somehow, to **slam on the brakes**, even though it's too late. Someone pulls me back.

"Hang on, Annika! Where are you going?" It's Johanna. "We've got a surprise for you. Stay right here!"

I look round. What kind of surprise? Johanna

---

to back away – den Rückzug antreten; fury – Wut;
to sneak off – davonschleichen;
to slam on the brakes – die Handbremse anziehen

manoeuvres me into a chair and all of a sudden, the room comes alive. They're dancing the "Time Warp" in my honour – it's the Rocky Horror Picture Show, except they're wearing slippers. Everyone joins in except Georg, who must have missed the rehearsals because he was ill. He looks at me from the opposite side of the room and tries to meet my eyes amid the singing and dancing **performers**. I think he wants to say sorry. Well, the damage has been done. My party is completely ruined. He should never have come. Now Mona hates me and everyone will blame me. They wouldn't be singing if they knew. I watch them more carefully. They look really professional. None of my old friends in Munich would put on a show like this. They've even changed the words to say something about "happy birthday" and "you're a star". I give Johanna a big hug. I know it was her idea. Tears are running down my face because of everything that's happened. "You're so sweet, Johanna. Thank you."

Johanna hugs me and holds me tight. It feels **comforting**. She pats my back **soothingly** and I feel her long hair brush against my neck. Jockel puts the music back on and everyone starts to dance. Suddenly Johanna whispers, "If I were a

---

performer – Künstler/-in; comforting – tröstlich; soothing – beruhigend

stone, I'd crumble before you. If I were a giant, I'd kneel at your feet. If I were the Rhine, I'd wrap myself around you and never let go."

My head starts throbbing and for a second it feels as though I'm in a vacuum. Everything seems quieter, slower, more distant. *J* stands for Johanna. Johanna is *J*.

Then the volume comes back again. I pull away from Johanna and stare at her.

"So it was *you*!"

She nods, smiles in embarrassment and bites her nails.

I honestly don't know what to do. I've had enough for one day. I look around for Mona, then remember that she hates me. I need someone to rescue me, but Mona has run off, Jockel is busy DJing and Georg has already caused too much trouble. If only I were invisible, then Johanna wouldn't be able to see me and neither would Georg or anyone else. Maybe if I were a vampire, I could fly away into the distance with a silent **screech**. But I'm just a lousy old human and I'll have to find something to say. "I'm sorry, Johanna. No one's ever done anything like this for me before. You're amazing. If only you were a guy ..."

"I get it." Johanna smiles back bravely.

I give her a quick hug, then disappear into the

---

screech – Schrei

kitchen and gulp down four sausages one after the next. I don't even bother with mustard. So it was Johanna all along. I must have been blind. Blind and stupid. Stupid and … in love with Georg.

"Annika, can we talk?"

I practically choke on my sausage. Georg has appeared out of nowhere. My cheeks go red with coughing and tears run down my cheeks. I can scarcely breathe.

"Has anyone seen the birthday girl?"

We both turn round. A good-looking guy is standing in the doorway. He's holding a **snow-globe** with a model of the television tower inside. He looks at me with his amazing dark eyes.

He smiles **wryly**. "I spotted your horns from the other room." He runs a hand through his shiny black hair and hands me his present. "Happy birthday!"

---

snow-globe – Schneekugel; wry – *hier:* schief

Mona, Alex, Johanna, Jockel, Suse, Georg and Me

Listen everyone: it's my birthday! You're supposed to be nice to me on my birthday. I'm tired of surprises. Anyone would think you've been trying to **wreck** my day.

I seem to have been standing here for hours. Alex is still holding the snow-globe, and I'm staring at him as though he's a reincarnation of the farmer's ghost. It takes an eternity for me to **compose** myself. "What are you doing here?"

"I wanted to give you this." He gives the globe a little shake and covers the television tower in snow. "And, uh, to talk."

His big dark eyes stare at me and I feel helpless at the sight of him. Then I remember how he hurt me. Besides, Georg wants to talk to me, too. He looks at me with his **stunning** green eyes. I can tell he's surprised to see Alex and he doesn't like it one bit. He looks him up and down, then he turns and faces me. It's the battle of the eyes. I feel as though

---

to wreck – ruinieren; to compose oneself – sich fassen; stunning – toll

I'm being **perforated** by brown and green lasers – I need to do something soon or I'll end up like a **sieve**. "You're not the only one," I say to Alex. "Everyone wants to talk to me but I only want to have fun. It's my birthday!" As if to prove it, I snatch up a burger and stuff it in my mouth. "Look, home-made burgers. You should try one."

Alex lowers the snow-globe and takes a step towards me. "Look, I'm sorry about what happened with Suse. My parents split up and I was feeling really down. Suse knows what it's like and ..."

"Are you **deaf** or something? She's not interested." Georg glares at Alex with his bright green laser eyes.

Alex fights back. "I don't mean to be rude, but it's none of your business."

"Oh yeah?" Green laser.

"Oh yeah." Brown laser.

"She said she's not interested." Green laser.

"What makes you so sure?" Brown laser.

"Shut up!" I yell at both of them. I turn to face Georg. "You shouldn't have told Mona. Not today."

I storm out of the kitchen. They've got no right to talk about me as if I'm not there. I slam the door and sigh. My feelings are a mess. I need to get away from all these crazy people who won't leave me

---

perforated – durchlöchert; sieve – Sieb; deaf – taub

alone. I almost reach the safety of my old bedroom when the phone starts ringing. I glance at the display – a Munich number. Oh God, it's Suse! I hesitate for a moment, wondering whether to let it ring. Then I remember that Suse is probably feeling the same way as me – guilty and wretched. I pick up the phone.

"Hi Suse," I **sob** into the receiver. "I guess you're calling because it's my birthday and you want to say sorry for what happened with Alex. You don't need to explain. I'm in the same situation. I can't talk right now but I'll call you tomorrow. I need to put things right."

The line goes quiet. I guess the conversation is taking Suse by surprise. "OK," she says softly.

"Great. Speak to you tomorrow!"

I hang up, stare at the phone and think about what I've said. *I need to put things right.* Yes, that's what really matters. I need to put things right with Mona.

"Annika! Where have you been?" Jockel runs down the stairs.

I grab my jacket and march out of the door. "I need to find Mona. Can you look after things here?"

Jockel nods. "I hope it works out."

I run out into rain, through the dark lifeless vil-

---

to sob – schluchzen

lage. I try to think of what to say. How can I explain things to Mona? I set her up with Georg, then ruined their relationship. I kissed her boyfriend. I need to find the right words but maybe there aren't any. My feet start to **drag**. Finally, I'm standing in front of the door. There's a light in the living room. I knock and wait nervously. I'm dripping with rain. The door opens. It's Mona's mum.

"Hello, Mrs Marthaler. Is Mona there?"

"She's in the cowshed. She volunteered to muck out the cows. Is it boy trouble or something?"

I nod.

"Oh dear, I remember what it's like. Maybe you can cheer her up a bit."

I try to smile. "Maybe."

I head for the cowshed. Cheer her up?! Thank God Mona's mum doesn't know what I've done. I peer through the window. It's hard to see anything through the dust, but I spot Mona **wielding** her **pitchfork**. It looks as though she's aiming for the Guinness Book of Records: Mona Marthaler, champion muck-clearer. Mona hates mucking out the cows! She's probably feeling empty and **drained**, just like I did. She's wearing all her old clothes and looks like the Mona I knew before we

---

to drag – *hier:* schlurfen; to wield – schwingen; pitchfork – Mistgabel; drained – leer, ausgelaugt

were friends. She won't want anything to do with me ever again. My stomach starts churning. There's only one way to stop it. I need to talk to her.

I open the door carefully but it still creaks like crazy. I bet everyone heard it across the village, in spite of the party. (A door creaks and everyone falls silent: listen everyone, ANNIKA'S GOING IN!) Mona glances up, but carries on determinedly. Her eyes are red with crying. "Hello," I say softly, closing the door behind me and taking a few nervous paces.

"You're welcome to him."

"I'm really sorry, Mona."

"I mean it. You can have him." Mona doesn't even look at me, just swings the pitchfork.

I stare at the floor and trace a **pattern** with my foot. "I'm not sure I want him any more. I was going to tell you, Mona, honestly I was. I'd decided to tell you tomorrow, when the party was over. But that idiot had to tell you straight away."

Mona gives one of the cows a little shove. "Get out of the way, Elsa!"

"Besides, you're more important to me. I'd give anything for you to forgive me."

"Out of my way, Elsa!"

"I'll tell Georg I'm not interested."

---

pattern – Muster

A forkful of dung lands in the **barrow**.

"I'll do your Latin homework for you."

No response.

"I'll muck the cows out every single day."

Mona vanishes behind Elsa. Silence. I couldn't feel lonelier if I were on the moon. Maybe I should go. Then I hear a mooing sound. It's Georg the calf. He's mooing at me. I walk over. This might be the last time I see him. I tickle him between the ears and he licks my hand. "I guess you'll give him a new name then."

"Why should I?" Mona's head pops up from behind Elsa. She glares at me, but I don't care: at least she's not ignoring me completely. "You can't blame the calf."

"I know," I say in a small voice. "It's all my fault." I try to smile. "Remember how we delivered him that night? I'll never forget it."

Mona stares at me.

"Take care, boy," I say sadly, giving Georg a final pat. Suddenly Mona appears alongside me. "Did you mean what you said about telling Georg you're not interested?"

I nod.

"But he's exactly your type. You're much better suited to him than me."

"So what?"

---

barrow – Schubkarre

Now it's Mona's turn to stroke Georg.

"Why does love have to be so complicated?" I sigh. "Why can't we just fall for one person and never split up?"

If only things could be that way. Then I'd still be with Alex, Mona would be with Georg, and everything would be fine.

"But if everyone stayed together for ever," says Mona, "I'd be the only one to kiss Georg … and that would be a **waste**, don't you think?"

I'm too surprised to speak. Never underestimate a village kid!

She grins, then pulls a serious face. "OK, four weeks."

"Pardon?" I don't know what she's talking about.

"You muck out the cows for four weeks, and I'll forgive you."

The **cheek** of it! I have to smile. "Two."

"Four, and Georg is yours."

"OK," I say and give her an enormous hug. Mona is unbelievable – the best friend in the world.

I walk across the farmyard, back to my party. All of a sudden, I feel like running. Mona decided to stay at home. I don't blame her – she's been through enough for one day.

---

waste – Verschwendung; cheek – Frechheit

I have to work out what to do about Georg. My feet are instantly **rooted** to the spot. What if he and Alex have had a duel? What if he's not interested any more? I run down the hill and nearly crash into him. He's been waiting for me on his moped. "Well?" he asks. His voice sounds almost normal.

"She forgave me."

Georg sighs with relief. "I couldn't face pretending any more." He looks at me tenderly. "And I was useless at it anyway."

"It's all right," I say, hugging my arms to my chest. What do we do now?

"Want to hear a horror story?" Georg looks at me expectantly.

I can't help grinning. I nod. Nothing can scare me after this evening.

"All aboard then!"

We drive through the **gloomy** village into the deserted countryside. It's drizzling. After a while we turn off the road on to a track and **wind** our way **up** a hill. We get to a **clearing**. Georg switches off the headlights and we're plunged into darkness. It takes a few seconds for my eyes to adjust. Georg leads me into the middle of a grassy area

---

to root – Wurzeln schlagen; gloomy – dunkel;
to wind up – nach oben winden;
clearing – Lichtung

surrounded by **looming fir trees** and enormous black boulders that look as though they've been thrown there by a giant's hand.

"The devil's rocks, I **presume**?"

Georg nods. "Remember the legend? This is where the devil met the maiden."

I swallow, look around and listen intently. No sign of any **demons**. "What happened to her?" I ask hoarsely.

"He seduced her," says Georg in a spooky voice, "and **condemned** her to hell!"

I stare at him.

"To be honest," he smiles, "he was probably just like me: an ordinary guy in love." He kisses me and I feel sure my heart is about to explode.

Hours and hours seem to pass. By the time we stop kissing, the rain has almost gone. The sky clears and the moon seems to shine just for us.

"Maybe we should go back," I say.

"If you want."

I do. It's my birthday and I ought to be celebrating with my guests.

The party is still going strong by the time we get home. Jockel has put on some slow music and is **waltzing** round the room with Johanna.

---

looming – drohend aufragend; fir tree – Fichte;
to presume – annehmen; demon – Dämon;
to condemn – verdammen; to waltz – Walzer tanzen

It didn't take Alex long to cope with my rejection. He's already in a tête-à-tête with some girl. She's wearing my clothes, and her hair is …

Oh my God! It's Mona! I thought she was nursing her broken heart at home …

Well, that's one thing I've learned here – village kids aren't as innocent as they seem!!

Ebenfalls auf Englisch bei Thienemann erschienen:

Sabine Both: *Move to Cloud Nine; Love in my Luggage*
Brinx/Kömmerling: *A Paul to Kiss*
Christamaria Fiedler: *Spaghetti Crime; Risotto Crime*
Sissi Flegel: *Forbidden to Love*
Bianka Minte-König: *Mobile Phone Love; Schoolyard Flirt & Catwalk Dreams*
Hortense Ullrich: *Never Kiss a Witch; Love is Blonde*
Zimmermann & Zimmermann: *Maths, Stress and a Lovesick Heart; School, Trouble & True Love Summer, Sun & Holiday Love*

Brinx/Kömmerling:
Country Boys, Country Love
Aus dem Deutschen von Sally-Ann Spencer
ISBN 978 3 522 17879 2

Reihengestaltung: Birgit Schössow
Einbandillustration: Birgit Schössow
Innentypografie: Marlis Killermann
Schrift: Stone serif
Satz: KCS GmbH, Buchholz/Hamburg
Reproduktion: Medienfabrik, Möglingen
Druck und Bindung: Friedrich Pustet, Regensburg

5 4 3 2 1* 07 08 09 10

www.thienemann.de
www.frechemaedchen.de